Empowering Learners

Empowering Learners

Teaching Different Genres and Texts to Diverse Student Bodies

Second Edition

Anna J. Small Roseboro
Susan B. Steffel

ROWMAN & LITTLEFIELD
Lanham • Boulder • New York • London

Published by Rowman & Littlefield
An imprint of The Rowman & Littlefield Publishing Group, Inc.
4501 Forbes Boulevard, Suite 200, Lanham, Maryland 20706
www.rowman.com

86-90 Paul Street, London EC2A 4NE, United Kingdom

British Library Cataloguing in Publication Information Available.

Library of Congress Cataloging-in-Publication Data Available
ISBN 9781475873030 (cloth : alk. paper) | ISBN 9781475873047 (pbk. : alk. paper) |
    ISBN 9781475873054 (ebook)

♾™ The paper used in this publication meets the minimum requirements of American
National Standard for Information Sciences—Permanence of Paper for Printed Library
Materials, ANSI/NISO Z39.48-1992.

We are grateful for the opportunity to reconnect and work together with other educators. Our goal is to empower those who are new to classroom teaching with the information, inspiration, and insight we gained in community with others during our decades in the profession. We dedicate this book

To those educators who teach adult college students and all the other educators who assist them as they begin the journey of earning a degree from an institution of higher learning.

To mentors and coaches seeking resources to support those colleagues new to the profession of education.

To all persons who are willing to share their knowledge and talents and who are ready to explore and expand their understanding of pedagogy in order to make their teaching the most effective it can be.

To persons who are seeking resources to plan effective and efficient use of in-class time to teach in a professional capacity.

Contents

Acknowledgments

–Claudia A. Marschall, who coauthored with Anna *Planning with Purpose: A Handbook for New College Teachers* (2021).

  –The eighteen contributors to this edition of this book. It is the generosity of gracious colleagues that makes this resource so rich.

  –Tom Koerner, Jasmine Holman, and David Bailey, Rowman & Littlefield editors, who accepted our proposal and oversaw the publication of this new edition.

  –We gratefully acknowledge our spouses, William Gerald Roseboro and Andrew Steffel, for their support to share what we have learned and to continue to learn with and from others who have devoted their careers to education.

We gratefully acknowledge the following endorsers for this book:

 –Gary Dohrer, professor emeritus at Weber State University, Ogden, Utah

  –Sarah J. Donovan, assistant professor of secondary English education, Oklahoma State University, Oklahoma City, Utah

  –Mursalta Muhammad, professor, Grand Rapids Community College, Grand Rapids, Michigan

  –Gretchen Rumohr, associate provost, director of The Center for Teaching Excellence, Aquinas College, Grand Rapids, Michigan

  –Deborah Van Duinen, associate professor, Hope College, Holland, Michigan

–Grover Welch, director of high school curriculum and adult learning, Newport Special School District, Newport, Arkansas

–Annette West, professor at Saint Leo University, St. Leo, Florida

–Joan Williams, retired English teacher, Arcata High School, Arcata, California

Introduction

"In learning you will teach, and in teaching, you will learn."[1]

–Phil Collins

Teaching is as much about inspiration as it is about information. You have been hired to teach because you know something but keeping in mind the fact that your students come knowing something, too, can make teaching a collaborative journey. Teachers are more than pitchers and students more than empty cups. This book is designed to share with you what we've learned about teaching different genres and texts to diverse student bodies, but we, Anna and Susan, don't come alone. Eighteen other colleagues have personally consented to share methods, materials, and management strategies, which we have woven into our text.

We come with decades of experience grounded in the research and proven pedagogy that we continue to learn throughout our academic careers and as active members of national professional organizations. As longtime members of the National Council of Teachers of English and the National Writing Project, and having served as presidents of our state affiliates, we have developed a love for teaching and are here to share what we have learned and experienced to help you develop success and satisfaction as classroom teachers, instructors, and professors.

WHO ARE WE TEACHING?

No matter the rigor of their precollegiate education, when they last studied, or where our students went to school, taking time to review the basics is a valuable way to use college class time. Once we discover, while doing focused

Allot time for students to turn and talk about texts.
https://www.istockphoto.com/photo/group-study-gm479608279-36252358

classroom activities, that our students are up to date on ways to access various genres of fiction, we know we can move ahead quickly to more academic reading that students may encounter in their other college coursework. So, we say, go ahead and start with short stories, move on to poetry, then dive into nonfiction and media.

Yes, media. So much messaging in the twenty-first century is visual and suggestive. If your students are alert to methods used to compel them to act or buy, they will be wiser and less likely to be drawn into behavior that is counterproductive to them as citizens in world culture.

WHAT ARE WE WRITING ABOUT?

The lessons are designed for those who know their academic subject matter but may have had little or no experience in teaching diverse students who may be high-school teens or adults many decades old, all in the same class. The chapters to come build on one another but can be read and utilized independently, and they present and expand on recommended pedagogy. These chapters are offered to support you as you frame lessons and design classroom experiences that enhance learning across the board.

Empowering Learners: Teaching Different Genres and Texts to Diverse Student Bodies describes ways to

- establish a nurturing classroom environment with firm but fair grading guidelines,
- plan in-class and homework assignments using strategies you can adopt or adapt, and
- balance student choice and teacher interest while meeting department goals and end-of-course content standards.

We encourage you to be alert to the settings in which our contributing colleagues teach, note the similarities to and differences from your classroom situation, and adapt accordingly. You will find

- samples of formative and summative assessments to measure student growth in learning,
- ways to select relevant print and media texts that serve as inspiration for living and patterns for writing and designing multimodal presentations,
- suggestions for assigning homework that extend and expand lessons you present in class and on virtual learning platforms, and
- lessons designed to engage adult students from various cultural, ethnic, and economic populations across the nation.

Most important, here are ideas to help you manage the load by sharing the burden in ways that permit both you, the instructor, and your students to see their progress in gaining the knowledge and refining the skills needed for success in the current course, classes that follow, and, later, in their jobs or career paths.

WHEN AND WHERE DO WE DEVELOP PROFESSIONAL PLATFORMS?

We are honored to have this opportunity to collaborate and share what we have learned in our several decades as classroom teachers with diverse student bodies.

Anna remains current regarding issues facing educators teaching students born in the twenty-first century. Most significantly, Anna has been cochair of the NCTE English Language Arts Teacher Educators (ELATE) Commission to Support Early Career English Language Arts Teachers and served many years with the NCTE Early Career Educators of Color program as a planner, mentor, co-director, and now is their emeritus mentor (2006–2023). She currently is one of the mentors for those seeking national board certification through the National Board for Professional Teaching Standards. In this publication, you will find an amalgamation of these teaching and learning experiences.

Equally relevant, Anna is the mother of an adult who was hired as a graduate assistant to teach introductory composition, primarily to first-year students. Much of what we share proved useful for her daughter's work and for others in her cohort during their years earning a master's degree in fine arts. Four of that cohort are among the seven new instructors who contributed to *Planning with Purpose: A Handbook for New College Teachers* (2021), which Anna coauthored with Claudia A. Marschall. Three of those new teachers, who have graduated and moved to different campuses, have contributed to our new book strategies they are refining and implementing with the students they currently teach.

Susan served as founding president of the Michigan Conference on English Education (a state affiliate of NCTE/CEE—now ELATE). She also served as coeditor of the award-winning *Language Arts Journal of Michigan* and was a founding director of the Chippewa River Writing Project. She has presented at the state, national, and international levels on topics including providing support for beginning teachers and incorporating classroom strategies to improve reading and writing. Her publications focus on the connections between reading and writing and using them to promote reading effectiveness across the curriculum with students of all ages.

In addition to her years of teaching at the university, Susan maintains connections with her former students and, when contacted with questions, continues to offer them advice and resources as they face the realities of their first classrooms. Her students often included nontraditional adult students, pursuing their education while balancing the responsibilities of families and other jobs. She works in and out of the classroom with diverse groups and individuals.

WHY KEEP READING?

Lessons in the upcoming chapters lay out strategies to help your students learn to read like writers. Sprinkled throughout is just enough theory and research background to provide an academic framework to help you understand why these strategies work. We know that educators who understand the "why" will be better able to tweak lesson plans to meet the needs of their particular students.

Here are guidelines for developing interactive in-class activities and for devising practical homework assignments. They are designed to better prepare your students to communicate with confidence in a variety of genres, rhetorical texts, and multimedia formats for diverse readers and viewers. The goals of the introductory, general-education courses in content areas, which are required courses at most institutions of higher learning, are to extend and expand understanding through exploration of the content in the curricula but not to result in experts after one course. Few students in your classes are aiming for an "A"; most of your learners just want to earn a high-enough grade in this class so they can get into the major of their choice. So, please resist being disappointed when all students do not strive for top grades. Do what you can to empower each of them to keep learning.

The main reason to keep reading is to discover what other veteran and novice educators of adults have to say about teaching reading. Our contributors are Kimberly Athans, Stefani Boutelier, Earl H. Brooks, Jim Burke, Sarah Hahn Campbell, José Louis Cano Jr., Shanika P. Carter, DuValle Daniel, Esther Gabay, Mara Lee Grayson, Cheryl Hogue Smith, Jessica Hudson, Nancy G. (Perkins) Kohl, Kia Jane Richmond, Rosalyn (Roz) Roseboro, Gayle Sands, Alison (Fastov) Taylor, and Anna White. Watch for their names and the settings in which they teach and note ways their ideas can be utilized with the students you teach.

HOW WILL MORE READING HELP?

What you learn can enable you to become an effective educator for whatever time you have to devote to classroom teaching. Please continue reading and learning ways our recommendations can guide, coach, support, and sustain you through your first years as an educator of adult college students. Explore ideas to develop and present lessons that meet your students' emotional and intellectual needs while challenging them to complete increasingly complex academic tasks. When students are learning, and you can document that learning through appropriate assessments, both you and your students enjoy more of your time together on the journey through each course of study.

Chapter One

Preplanning for Effective Use of Class Time

Lessons in the upcoming chapters lay out strategies to teach your students to read like writers. We offer guidelines to develop collaborative in-class activities and to devise practical homework assignments to better prepare your students to communicate with confidence in a variety of genres, rhetorical texts, and multimedia formats for diverse readers and viewers.

The course goals of introductory, general-education classes in content areas that are required at most institutions of higher learning are designed to extend and expand student knowledge through the exploration of the curricula content but not to produce experts after one course. Few students come aiming for an "A"; most of your learners just want to earn a high-enough grade so they can get into the major of their choice. So, please resist being disappointed when all students do not strive for top grades. Do what you can to empower each of them to keep learning.

In an article in the blog *Higher Ed Gamma*, Steven Mintz encourages college instructors to do the following:

1. *Focus on outcomes, not just courses.* It's what students know and can do, not just their grades, that matters. Concentrate more, then, on student learning and do more to drive their improvement by providing more timely feedback and constructive criticism.
2. *Educate students for life, not just in a discipline-specific major.* Relatively few college graduates pursue a career that is tightly aligned with their major. Therefore, it's essential to ensure that our alumni be well prepared for all that lies ahead, both professionally and personally.[1]

Satisfactory experiences in a particular class may entice some students to seek a major in that subject. More, however, will simply gain a deeper appreciation for folks like you, who empowered them to understand more of what they read and to write with more confidence about what they are learning.

As a general prewriting strategy, the lessons will be framed so students can answer questions like these.

1. In the different genres and texts we have been reading, how have the writers structured their writing to keep readers reading?
2. What do you want your readers to know and be able to do when they have read and reflected on what you have written?
3. How did the authors whose work we've been reading establish their credibility?
4. How can you establish your own credibility as the author of your writing?
5. What patterns will you use in this writing to invite, inform, and impress your writers enough to keep them reading?

Descriptions of in-class and homework assignments in the upcoming chapters point out successful strategies that encourage students to reflect on both the published selections and the unpublished drafts of their peers. In so doing, your learners will be developing a sense of what clarifies and what clouds the messages in their own writing. Questions like the ones above will

Planning for classroom teaching need not overwhelm you.
https://www.istockphoto.com/photo/worried-and-bored-student-gm862314614-142924675

help students to write clearer, more engaging examples of the genres and texts you are teaching.

CONSIDER THE TIME FOR TIMING

Plan lesson presentations based on the day of the week, the time of the day, and the length of your class meeting. You know that classes that meet on Mondays and Wednesdays have a different energy level than those that meet on Tuesdays and Thursdays. You know that classes that start at 8 a.m. and 4 p.m. have different rhythms. Classes that meet for two hours and those that meet once a week for three hours must be structured differently. No matter the day of the week, time of day, or hours that you meet, know that adults' attention span is generally thirteen to fifteen minutes. So, plan accordingly.

A general rule of thumb is to have written lesson plans that include these four "P's": *prepare*, *present*, *practice*, and *ponder*. Students *practice* something they are learning in class (perhaps modeling something introduced in the recent class), *prepare* something needed to participate actively in the next class meeting (research, view, read, collaborate), *polish* a presentation for the next class or soon-to-come meeting (oral, virtual, dramatic), and students *ponder* by doing self-reflections on their performance on a recent assignment or thinking about what they plan to do better on the next assignment or in the next course. A variety of charts for lesson planning are online. All will have similar components, and we encourage you to use a formal lesson plan for the first full course that you teach. Choose the template or layout that works for you but know that purposeful planning prepares you to effectively use the time for which students are paying tuition. You can be assured that they will be getting good value for their money.

HONOR CULTURAL HOLIDAYS

Equally important is to know and honor the times of cultural holidays your students and their families observe and celebrate, including hallowed holidays like Chinese New Year, Christmas, Easter, Passover, and Ramadan. Many distinctive holidays include family gatherings or fasting. Even if your students are not home, memories may drain their attention, time, and energy and impact your learners' ability to complete assignments with care. Be aware, too, that some students celebrate no religious holidays.

Opening Class with a Focus for the Day

Prepare students for the lesson to come with an opening activity as a warm-up or focus strategy. No matter what the students have been doing before they arrive for your class, they need to focus on something specific to be attentive during the time they will be spending with you. This could be as simple as a posed question, a focused free writing time, or a prepared slide that engages the students and readies them for the day's lesson. Within your lesson plan, purposefully plan twenty-minute chunks that include time to talk and move.

1. Present the lesson for the day in twelve to fourteen minutes.
2. Provide a practice activity where students actually use the information or skill you have just presented. Successful pedagogies have "I do it," "We do it," "They do it" components.
   a. (I) You, the teacher, instruct and show students what and how to use information or strategy.
   b. (We) Together, you and the students, do something with that information or strategy.
   c. (They) Have students work together in pairs or small groups to utilize that information or strategy.

Showing Rather Than Just Telling

We find that it's helpful for each class meeting to have a set of slides prepared for each segment of the lesson. Some educators have the slides with the plan for the day scrolling as students come into the room. Make the slides (three to four sets that repeat for two to three minutes). You may find that having music playing while the slides are scrolling will help set the "tone" for the day. Some educators have the same song playing for a full unit. Others may select a song that fits the text or topic being studied that day. Some instructors later invite students to bring in music to be played as class starter songs or for in-class writing time.

Music can make a positive difference in nurturing active learning. Be aware that some students can be very distracted by sounds and music, so it is good practice to survey the class to learn the needs of your students.

Arrive at your classroom as early as you can. If you're sharing a room, honor the time of the person there, but let your colleague know you'd like to get set up while he or she is clearing up. Set your slides to be running two minutes before your class period begins. This way, you can meet and greet your students at the door.

Once the class period begins officially, direct students' attention to the slides with the overview or plan for that class meeting and explain why you are using them. By knowing what's coming, students will know that you are prepared and that they must be open to learning.

Present the new idea, theory, application, or text. *Show* the students how to apply what you just told them. Have an activity planned for students to do something *together* first, then independently. This individual activity is pondering time during which students reflect on what they have just learned and have been asked to do.

Flexible Pacing Keeps All on Task

Guided talk teaches. However, consider having the students write something to capture their understanding and then talk with a partner or those seated at the same table about what you have just presented. This "pair-and-share" activity allows you to evaluate their understanding easily. Stroll around the classroom, listening and learning.

To stay on pace, consider inserting timers into your slides that alert you and the students to move on. The sounds need not be startling but should be loud enough to be heard throughout the space in which you are working. For example, when you have completed your twelve-to-fourteen-minute presentation, set a timer for three to five minutes for students to write a summary of what you've presented and a response to a prompt you have projected. Following are examples:

1. What three things did you learn about today?
2. How can you see this idea, skill, or concept being used in another setting?
3. What questions do you still have about what we're working on today?

When the buzzer rings, have the students *turn* to their peers and *talk*, using their notes as guides for that conversation.

You may have a short text that exemplifies the literary technique, rhetorical device, or organizational pattern you've just talked about. Allot time for students to read that sample and apply the unlocking strategy that you've just demonstrated. Then they should turn to and talk with their peers about what they discovered in applying what you've just taught.

Set the timer for five to seven minutes of small group discussion. You may find yourself adjusting the timing based on the efficiency of their talking. Giving them prompts to begin their conversations helps but should not limit them.

Random Groupings Help Expand Learning

A randomizing strategy could be as simple as having students write the final four numbers of their cell phone number. Add the digits and circle the first number in the sum. That number will be the group they will be in for this activity. The students may giggle or appear hesitant, but that's okay. You're asking them to think and then move. That's okay, too.

Another grouping strategy is the ABC summary whereby students summarize the reading done for homework by creating sentences that begin with their assigned letters of the alphabet: group 1 corresponds to A to E; group 2 to F to J; group 3 to K to O; group 4 to P to T; and group 5 to U to Z

First, set a timer and invite students to write their own ABC sentences in three to five minutes, then meet in their groups for five to seven minutes to come up with a group summary with sentences beginning with their assigned letters. Then, you call, in numerical order, the groups, and their chosen spokesperson reads aloud the sentences that their group has written.

In fewer than twenty minutes, your students will have reflected, pondered, written, and talked through a complex reading. You will have been circulating among the writers and discussants, and you now know how well they comprehend the text, as well as what you may need to review or expand on before moving forward.

Do you want even more grouping strategies? No worries. You can find myriad online randomizers you can utilize over the weeks you meet with these students. You simply need to have a class list that you can copy and paste into the app.

Closing Class Methodically

Close each class meeting in an orderly way. Have a timer set for five minutes before the end of the class meeting. First, draw students' attention to the slides you project as you review what has been taught, then move on to summarize what you've observed during their working together. Next, give homework assignments that will be due at the next class meeting, and, finally, show students the location on the class learning platform so the students can find the instructions for the resources you've stored there for their use.

If appropriate for that day's lesson, post questions or prompts that invite or require students to write and send you three takeaways for the day.

1. What is something new you learned or understood better today?
2. What questions do you still have?
3. How can you apply what we discussed today to another college or work setting?
4. What more do you wish to learn about this subject?

Have students send the note to your school email address *before* they leave class.

With careful planning, your students will progress through the course with confidence that you are empowering them to meet the course standards set by the college or university in which they are enrolled.

TRAVEL PLAN FOR ACCESSING TEXTBOOKS

If you are teaching first-year college students, especially during the first semester, consider adding a "How to Use Your Textbook" lesson during the second week of the course. Invite students to bring to class a textbook for a history, social science, or math class or for any other class they are taking for which they are required to have a printed textbook.

Plan a scavenger hunt to find common textbook features in random order, not in the order in which they generally appear in the book. Make it a "fun" activity that takes only fifteen minutes or so of class time. Ask students to sit on their books while you are presenting the WHY and HOW of the lesson. They'll think it's weird or fun. You know they will more likely be paying attention, wondering what you're going to have them do next.

Orderly closings reflect, clarify, and project on learning.
https://www.istockphoto.com/photo/male-college-tutor-with-digital-tablet-teaching-class-gm876961880
-244742217

As with other frame lessons, those that are firmly structured, with flex built in, begin by sharing with the students the WHY of the scavenger hunt. One WHY is to show them how the authors of their textbooks use many of the strategies they are learning in this course. Give students the list of typical textbook features, then invite small groups to prepare and present the function of each section.

Group the students by the kind of textbook they have. Then prompt them with questions that send them to various support sections of the book and the visuals that further expand the text. The most common text features of a book include the table of contents, the index, headings, captions, bold words, illustrations, photographs, the glossary, labels, graphs, charts, and diagrams. Not all books use all of these, so it is another good discussion to talk about which features are used for which books.

Then invite students, individually, to read a section of their textbook and describe the rhetorical features of that page: expository, compare/contrast, persuasive, key sign words as transitions, and PIE paragraphs (P is for position or opinion, I and E are for illustrate with examples), as described in chapter 2.

You could have students do a "romp through the book," similar to that activity described in chapter 2, answering the questions that follow. Instruct students to turn to a randomly chosen page and list what text features are on that page. Instruct them next to go to the glossary and locate and write down words that begin with five different letters found in the student's own name. Students should ask themselves which of those words are new and what those new words mean. Instruct students to then find an illustration and to ask themselves whether it is of a person, an event, or something else. Instruct them to locate a sentence on the page, other than the caption, that the student can link to that graphic, chart, map, or picture.

Continue, as time permits, by asking questions like these. Are there captions under the diagrams? What additional information do those captions provide for the reader? Instruct students to look in the table of contents. Which chapter is about a subject they studied in high school? About seven minutes into the hunt, call time and ask students to turn to a page that is at least two-thirds text. Now you will bridge this activity into the content in your class. Ask them to read that page and identify the rhetorical devices, organization patterns, key signal words, and other features they find in their textbook.

Knowing they know how to navigate this important print resource will give students more confidence and increase their likelihood of success in other courses. Learning to utilize such textbook features more efficiently may be credited to the reading and learning they'll be doing in your class.

PREP FOR RESEARCH: JUST AS, SO TOO

As you consider lessons to teach students to do something specific, consider what the skill is like. For example, when you assign students to include in their persuasive essays opinions of experts, plan and present a lesson that reminds students of what they do to search for information on the internet. But, don't tell them; show them.

Anna White, a member of the library staff at Grand Valley State University in Michigan, does a quirky lesson that gets the students all excited. She brings in a unique shoe and asks the students to "research" and find out as much different information as they can about that particular shoe. This lesson demonstrates to students the importance of trying different keywords when searching for sources. You could have students navigate to Amazon's website. Display the image of a very specific item (that you've found prior to class) and ask them to do searches until they find the item. Once someone has found it, ask which key words they used to find it.

Then you can show how a similar approach—trying more general or more specific key words—is necessary when searching on a library database.

It is not until the end of the class that Anna White adds the "just as, so too" element of instruction. She generally points out that, just as students refined their search using specific terminology and jargon to learn about this shoe, so too can they do the same when conducting research for and about the reading and writing for their college courses.

CHECK OUT RESOURCES FOR SUPPLIES

Check with your department about the availability of supplies like markers, index cards, colored paper, snacks, and similar items. Small grants might be available for classroom projects through the department, the college, or the library. Check around.

If you're teaching in a place where you regularly attend a house of worship or are in a sorority or fraternity, invite them to help. Ask them to support your work as an educator by donating bags of wrapped hard candy. Again, folks may smile and wonder, so tell them what you're doing and why. Someone will come through for you. Consider, too, requesting contributions from local businesspersons. Many local business organizations have budgets to support the education of people in their community. Consider Rotary, Kiwanis, Lions, and Optimist clubs. You may be surprised how family members will donate to support your work, too. We have not because we ask not.

CONCLUSION

In summary, plan carefully, with flexibility built in. Know what main idea, concept, or skill you intend to teach in each class meeting. Plan four P strategies (prepare, present, practice, and ponder) appropriate for the day and time your class meets. Begin with a warm-up or starting activity to provide focus or create intrigue about the lesson for the day. Work out twenty-minute chunks during which you first show or model a strategy for reading and then you have your learners work together in pairs or groups and then apply the strategy independently, on their own. Include time for purposeful movement, if nothing more than standing up and stretching before sitting down and reading or writing. Movement remotivates.

Chapter Two

Laying the Roadbed for Smoother Travel

Educators in the humanities often hear the Rudine Sims-Bishop expression that books can serve as windows or mirrors or both. This is true, but, along the education journey, quagmires can bog down inexperienced teachers who think this concept is an "either/or" situation. Some believe that, if the text is by someone of the same race, religion, or region as the readers, the text will be a mirror; if the author is different from the student, the reading experience will be a view through a window. But that seldom is the case because a single author does not speak for, or to, every one of his or her ethnic or social group.

A distinctive experience opened Anna's eyes when she assumed that reading a writing by an African American, Toni Morrison, would be a wide-open window experience for European American students in Anna's class.

TELLING PERSONAL STORY ILLUSTRATES THE FACT

For a culminating assignment one year, Anna's students got to choose an author who had won a prestigious writing award during the students' lifetime. One Caucasian student selected Toni Morrison and chose to read *The Bluest Eye*.

On the day of her oral presentation, the student held up the requisite visual aid. In her case, it was a poster depicting large bright-blue eyes with dilated pupils in which she had drawn a picture of herself. From one eye dripped a faint trail of tears.

You may know that Pecola, the main character in the Morrison novel, is a young African American girl with low self-esteem, the victim of verbal and physical bullying, who believes she is ugly. She thinks she can be beautiful only if she were to have blue eyes. She tries various strategies to change her physical appearance to better fit that norm of beauty and, in doing so, becomes mentally deranged.

The European American student saw herself in Pecola but in a much different way. This teenager had accepted a social norm that being thin is a sign of physical beauty, and she nearly killed herself by not eating. Subsequent emotional and physical distress led to hospitalization for anorexia. Thankfully, medical attention and counseling helped her overcome those feelings of self-hate. Reading during her recovery, the young lady related in her report that she identified with Pecola's pain. But, unlike the fictional character, this student returned to emotional and physical health and to class where she shared her story. Before she finished her report, most of the listeners became as teary as her visual depiction of weeping blue eyes.

This experience illustrates the assertion of Rudine Sims Bishop who wrote, "When lighting conditions are just right, however, a window can also be a mirror. Literature transforms human experience and reflects it back to us, and in that reflection, we can see our own lives and experiences as part of a larger human experience."[1] You can be the light for your students; they also can be light for you.

Books can serve as a mirror in the least expected ways. We, educators, cannot preclude or predict the power of a text for our students. In other words, any book may be a window or a mirror or both to any student. So, when you have the option to select texts, choose them because they are well written; let the authors speak for themselves, and allow students to choose, write, and talk about what the texts say or reveal to them.

The challenge, of course, will be designing lessons that help learners understand how authors use words, sentence structure, and order to tell their stories and make their cases. Learning the language of literature and rhetorical devices will help students understand the strategies used and acquire a vocabulary to discuss fiction, nonfiction, and visual literature and texts by diverse authors.

In the chapters to come there will be strategies for using class time, designing homework assignments, and creating formative and summative assessments for your students. As you review and model, then give students opportunities to practice using these terms in conversation and writing, also consider opportunities for them to draft and share their own stories. To be able to read is a good thing; to comprehend what one reads is better; to explore how different genres and texts work just expands that enlightening experience of reading.

SETTING THE GROUNDWORK FOR
OPEN CONVERSATIONS

To make this a positive instructional experience for you and your students, consider ways you can incorporate *writing to learn* into your course. In this writing, students explain, explore, and expand their thinking about the texts you assign, but you only need to read what they write, not grade it for correctness. This *writing to learn* serves multiple purposes in an English course.

One benefit of *writing to learn* is helping students prepare to talk with their peers and in class discussion. The strategy may be one you know already: "think, pair, share" or "turn and talk." Just allow a few moments for students to write before they are expected to verbalize their thinking. This teaching strategy is particularly useful in classes with students who are shy, new to the college, or English-language learners.

Writing to Explore, Explain, and Expand Reading

Many students can read and understand quite well when they have dictionaries nearby and access to the internet when they read. But, for international students, being asked to verbalize their thinking without having time to access the words in English, arrange them in their minds, and figure out how to pronounce the words understandably evokes near trauma for them. On the other hand, if you allow a couple minutes for all students to write a few words, phrases, or sentences, those who need a little more time to organize their thinking will be prepared to share their insights with more confidence.

Understanding Students of Different Backgrounds

In courses with adults, their different ages, prior experiences, and familiarity with college settings may all be reasons to provide them with additional skills for reading more complex texts and writing for academic readers. So, there is no need to hesitate. Knowing their benefit, offer as prompts sentence starters like these: "This makes me think of . . . "; "It surprised me when . . . "; and "I wonder why . . .." Your international students, those who have recently arrived in the country and are not yet accustomed to speaking and writing in English, will appreciate this kind of linguistic support, too, and the additional time to process their thoughts before being required to verbalize them.

Those who are teaching adults in college settings will find spans of understanding but for different reasons. Some of your students will have just completed enriched high-school classes with much talking and writing about texts. Others may be significantly older adults returning to school after years away from academic coursework. Many in the two-year college setting may be adults who have completed a General Educational Development (GED) test to qualify for freshman English. This range of students may be in the same class. So, thoughtful classroom teachers, graduate students, and adjunct professors conscientiously model talking about texts for all students because it reminds those who know the literary terminology and begins teaching those who do not . . . yet.

Your acclimating students will soon be able to recognize and discuss themes on a more abstract level, once they are reminded of what they're looking for. Consider posting or projecting prompts, such as:

1. In this piece of literature, what is it about the conflict and response to it that would be true, regardless of time or place? (Universality.)
2. What incidents in the beginning, middle, and end of this piece suggest that yours is a valid theme statement? (To validate their observation, ask for quotations, direct references, and page numbers.)
3. What role(s) do(es) certain character(s) play in revealing that theme? (Recognizing the role of major and minor characters.)
4. Where have you seen similar behavior in literature and in life? (Validating observation, making connections to what they have read, seen, or experienced.)

Less-experienced readers probably will be fine with S.W.B.S.T. strategy. They may recall from middle or high school describing the events in a story using the prompt "somebody wanted, but, so, then." Ask them if they remember . . . or teach it to them. Modulate to more sophisticated structures as students mature.

Go ahead and accept any theme statement that can be validated, even if it seems far-fetched on first hearing. Accepting new but verifiable theme statements encourages students to think for themselves, knowing they will be required to support their opinions with direct references from the texts.

Enjoy this time with your students as you implement activities that help these learners probe more deeply and understand more fully the beauty of writing and the joy of reading.

Adapting Literature Circles

Literature circles, a discussion strategy attributed to Harvey "Smokey" Daniels, is an effective way to get students to interact with texts from different perspectives. Daniels describes five basic roles: summarizer, illustrator, travel tracer, word wizard, and connector.[2] Once modeled, this strategy works well with students from a variety of cultures and with various degrees of ease with language! Check out online discussions of this strategy for ways to structure a unit that rotates roles, so all readers have an opportunity to experience each of the roles . . . once they see you demonstrate them.

Consider modeling one or two roles during consecutive class meetings when students begin reading a new assigned book. Then, share a video that describes the roles for them to view as homework. Be prepared to review that video in the next class meeting, and then have students practice with each other. Yes, starting books together tends to get students off to a more solid start. You could post a couple of guiding questions on the board to remind students to pay attention to elements of exposition they will find in the opening chapter(s) of their novels. Then allow twenty minutes for them to read. Perhaps you can begin by reading the first chapter aloud or read to them for ten minutes, giving the rest of the time for independent reading. Having that short, initial taste is sometimes just enough to pique their interest and make them eager to continue on their own. However, once you complete the exposition, encourage them to read at their own pace. Consider comparable steps for reading nonfiction, too.

MEASURING WITH NINE YARDSTICKS OF VALUE

Teaching a general set of criteria early in the course can help you build a safe place with freedom for honesty in your classroom. Introducing guidelines for evaluating and responding to literature frees students to write definitively about texts they do not like with as much confidence as writing about texts they thoroughly enjoy.

In some precollegiate settings, students had to look at literature in only a quantitative way, learning elements of fiction—*characters, setting, plot, conflict, theme*, etc.—and may even have written some critical analyses. The next step is to look at literature in a qualitative way, developing a sounder and more defensible conclusion, and seeing traits in literary works students may otherwise miss. Knowledge of such standards, in short, makes for thoughtful evaluations that will be more satisfying to students and more compelling to their classmates. In these lessons, we will call these standards "yardsticks."

Those teaching freshman college courses will find reviewing or teaching these yardsticks to be an efficient way to assess what students already know. They will help you discover what you must teach for your students to be able to meet the standards or outcome goals of your course. Once you have a good idea of who knows what, you can adjust the pace of future lessons.

Consider adapting the *nine yardsticks of value* originally described in a literature text by Blair and Gerber. These educators suggest that students consider the elements of clarity, escape, reflection of real life, artistic details,

internal consistency, tone, personal beliefs, emotional impact, and significant insights.

Working as a class, ask students to score their response to a text or video
they already have studied together. Try to mask your own opinions as students
add their comments as they talk about the following:

- CLARITY: how easy or difficult the text or media was to understand
  when students read or viewed it
- ESCAPE: how much students found themselves drawn away from their
  everyday life as they read the text or viewed the media
- REFLECTION OF REAL LIFE: how much the people and places
  seemed familiar or reflect life as students know it
- ARTISTRY IN DETAILS: whether students found the selection engaging enough to reread or review, whether the author used fresh imagery,
  realistic dialogue, or "sparkling" vocabulary that made readers pause
  and bask in the beauty of the passage or scene (similar criteria may
  be applied to a director's use of camera angles and shots, lighting,
  and music)
- INTERNAL CONSISTENCY: if the text or video flows well and all parts
  seem to fit in a meaningful way, and if, on the other hand, either seems
  disjointed or has scenes that could be deleted without being missed
- TONE: how well an author's tone, personal style, or attitude comes
  through the composition (some may rate highly the selection that creates
  a strong emotional response, whether it is a positive or negative one)
- PERSONAL BELIEFS: to what degree the text or video confirms personal beliefs (even if readers cannot articulate their reactions, all are
  influenced by their own ideas relating to religion, politics, social issues,
  and attitudes about what is moral or immoral, right or wrong)
- SIGNIFICANT INSIGHT: whether the composition provides a window
  to and a mirror of life, offering new insight into individuals, groups,
  places, and situations (possibly compelling those who experience it
  to consider their own behaviors and thoughts about life and death,
  good and evil)

The "significant insight yardstick" is especially challenging as college students begin to experience more culturally diverse texts than they may have
encountered earlier. But don't let that stop you from offering students the
opportunity to evaluate print and media texts using these nine yardsticks of
value. See the Nine Yardsticks of Value chart in chapter 6 on which students
can be asked to rate from one to five (low to high) their evaluation of the
reading. Using these ratings, they can talk and write based on their response
to the text.

It may take several class meetings to introduce all of the yardsticks, but doing so can help students to

- see the sequential nature of their reading skills,
- discover reasons for their own responses to various genres,
- expand their vocabulary for discussing and writing about texts, and
- read and analyze published literary criticism more insightfully,

all while becoming more open-minded, freer to write honestly, and more willing to allow the creativity of complex writers to draw them in, amaze and inform them as these learners become more open-minded to what they read and what they write.

Instructors of adults will find it useful to remind students that they are likely to have been taught similar approaches to text while in high school. Inviting students to share with classmates the strategies they recall will empower the learners and reinforce the fact that all in the classroom can learn from one another. So, please know that efficient, successful teachers take time for such review and sharing before moving on to more sophisticated language that asks students to explore various texts from multiple perspectives in order to gain deeper understanding of the writers' method and message.

INTERROGATING TEXTS

Cheryl Hogue Smith teaches at a community college in a large urban city. Her students often work full-time or at least work several hours part-time, traveling on public transportation to and from school for one-to-two hours each way. Many also have extensive family obligations, are food or housing insecure (or both), and frequently deal with life circumstances that under-standably interfere with or take precedence over their learning.

One exercise Smith uses to teach reading is "interrogating texts," in which students are asked to write individually their responses to open-ended questions about their experiences with a text they are reading and to read aloud their responses to each other before any group discussion starts. By not being able to defer to or parrot someone else's response, they learn to trust their own ideas; for some, this is the first time they have realized that their thinking has merit.

In practice, "interrogating texts" divides a course reading into parts, and the directions for each part are usually identical. The first question in each of the parts asks students to do the following:

1. On your own, silently reread the [first/second/third] section of the text.

2. Based upon your reading of this portion of the text, paraphrase what you think the author is saying.
3. After you paraphrase the text, write down any questions that this portion of the text leaves you with, and try to answer those questions.

Smith says, "I ask students to first paraphrase a text in order to have them read for understanding, focusing solely on what they think the passage says. Only after all students read their responses aloud do they then discuss their responses and write down anything new or interesting they learned from their group mates." She strives to get students to write what they think so they can read—and learn to trust in—their responses.

Once students complete the first direction, Smith has them move on to part two of the same section of text:

1. Reread the same section, one more time, and underline the one sentence that you think is most important to the meaning of the entire section.
2. Explain why you think this one sentence is the most important sentence in the piece.
3. If you found some of this text difficult, mark what you think were the most confusing parts, and discuss these with your group.

The direction to explain why that one sentence is the "most important to the meaning of the entire section" is deliberately vague so students can interpret the question in whatever way makes sense to them.

Again, by reading their responses before any discussion begins, students learn that they are capable readers and that they can support their interpretations of texts with evidence from those texts, especially in negotiations with readers who disagree with them. Sometimes a portion of an assigned text is so difficult and crucial to the meaning of the entire piece that Smith adds a third kind of question that leads students through more guided, rather than open-ended questions.

LEARNING THE LANGUAGE OF THE LAND

You know the value of a broad, rich vocabulary, even if you visit just a different area of the nation and not some exotic country on a different continent. The same is true for your students. For many, the language of college may seem just as foreign. As you scope out the journey of the courses you teach, know that your students will need to understand some basic terms to be able to follow directions and stay on task. You can plan from the very beginning to teach vocabulary intentionally, without having to drill students, allowing them to acquire the skill of recognizing and using more sophisticated language in and out of class. If they use it, they won't lose it.

Consider levels of vocabulary. As you choose and prepare lessons around specific readings, select and provide definitions for words that are specific to that book or article. These are words that the reader must understand to comprehend the piece. Then there are also those words that are just vocabulary expanders. Such words may not be critical to readers' understanding but are words unfamiliar to them.

It also is helpful to pull out some of the vocabulary specific to the genre or academic field, in this case the field of literature, that students will need to know across the content areas. Don't go overboard. I remember being overwhelmed by vocabulary lists, and your students will be, too. It is important to limit this list. Perhaps you can focus on five words from each level of vocabulary or five-five-five. The focus should be on the text in its entirety, not the individual words.

You may recognize these levels of vocabulary as corresponding to Tier 1, 2, and 3 words, terms based on how practical the words are for one or more of the following: everyday speaking, reading, writing, and academic use. In your area of the country, you may hear about the "forty-forty-forty" rule, which refers to words students need to know—for forty days, forty weeks, or forty years—and then allot teaching and study time accordingly. As we've discussed before, people's core vocabularies differ widely. Depending on the makeup of your class, another way to approach vocabulary in literature is to direct students to keep their own list of those words that "bump them out" of the reading.

Vocabulary is definitely an important aspect of reading, but every day we each read print without stopping to look up every unknown word. Reading is about predicting what's coming next, and, as long as our predictions keep working, we continue. It's only when we come to something that suddenly doesn't conform to our prediction or doesn't make sense that we're forced to look up a word or backtrack in our reading.

So, if students merely jot down or highlight an unfamiliar or interesting word while they're reading, not stopping to look it up unless doing so is necessary for understanding, they will have a personal list of their own. You could share those words in a classroom list or word cloud to see how many others selected them or leave them discrete. Regardless of how you choose to handle vocabulary, we urge you again to use restraint. Learning vocabulary is a means to understanding the whole. It is not the goal itself.

Think about creating a virtual "word wall" that you project for students to see specific words as the course unfolds. Add to or change the list to coordinate with the texts you are teaching. On discussion or writing days, draw students' attention to the list and encourage them to incorporate this vocabulary as they talk and write. General words can be in one color font and specific words in another. Fresh lists create new interest just as the changing road signs you notice along the highway revive interest in the trip. Those teaching in virtual settings can create hyperlinks that students can click on to get them to these "word walls." The key is to make it easy for students to access what they need to learn in order to do well in the course.

Among the academic words to begin defining and using in early lessons are those having to do with instructions: explain, diagram, evaluate, describe, analyze, discuss, and so on. If your students are new to academic work in English, they may have different ideas about what is required when asked to do these tasks. Help your fellow travelers get off to a good start by clarifying what is expected when they see or hear these terms. You can find lists of academic words on websites describing Bloom's taxonomy verbs to help you measure students' level of knowledge, comprehension, application, analysis, synthesis, evaluation, and creativity.

Once settled into your classes, you may want to present a lesson on the different definitions the same word may have in different content areas. For instance, the word *plot* in English refers to an element of fiction; in social studies' map reading or in history, it may be a *plot* of land or *to plot* a course of action; and, in science or math, it may be *to plot* a graph. The word *draw* is another of those words with multiple definitions. Review those terms in light of your course and give succinct examples of what you would expect to see when you assess student learning.

After vocabulary is taught, add the goal of using vocabulary words to your customized rubrics. For example, when writing the final paper about a major work, include a requirement that students incorporate smoothly in their writing between eight and ten vocabulary words from the recent vocabulary list. Later in the course, include use of literary terms and rhetorical devices in the requirements for a paper or product that earns a passing grade.

TEACHING VOCABULARY BEFORE, DURING, AND AFTER READING

Students should feel free to use internet websites as they read assigned texts. Model this practice for your students early in the course. Before they encounter them in the text, remind students how to search for vocabulary words on the list you have prepared. Then click on "images" to demonstrate how both the denotation and various connotations of the words often appear. This may be all they need to be able to read with more depth and understanding about a topic completely foreign to their experiences. It may be particularly easy if they are using an e-reader device that provides definitions, and you

Read-around groups—an option for peer feedback.
https://www.istockphoto.com/photo/wide-angle-view-of-high-school-students-sitting-at-desks-in-classroom
-using-laptops-gm1133836004-301077276

can demonstrate that as well. The more diverse your student body, the more important it is to implement a variety of strategies to enhance your teaching and student learning.

GETTING INTO THE READING

Are you familiar with the "into, through, and beyond" strategy for teaching text? Looking for something that can work in a single period to get students into their next book? Keeping in mind that students from different cultures may respond differently but validly to these strategies, here are a few ideas to consider.

Design a Random Romp through the Book

First, direct students to open their journals. Then, direct them to open their books and do the following activities:

- Write in their journals any ten numbers corresponding to any page from page one to the last page in the book
- Turn to and skim those ten pages

- Copy sentences from five of those pages (one each) that catch their attention because they seem
  - interesting
  - surprising
  - provocative
  - confusing
- In a short paragraph, write what they think these sentences say about the book's characters, setting, conflict, or topic or the position the author is taking in a nonfiction text (remember, reading is about predicting)

Give the students a few minutes to share with one another their chosen sentences and to talk briefly about similarities and differences in their inferences about the book. Consider having students return to these notes later to compare their before and after ideas about the text.

Resist the temptation to make comments yourself. The goal here is to spark curiosity and inspire students to read to find their own answers.

Now, begin the book together with you (the teacher) dramatically reading aloud for them or playing an audible version of the opening pages for five-to-seven minutes; stop and let students continue reading until five minutes before the class period ends. During the final five minutes, give your learners an "exit slip" assignment in which they answer the following questions:

1. What have you learned?
2. What do you expect to happen next?
3. What puzzles or confuses you?

If students have electronic devices available, they can tweet, email you, or post to Padlet, Google Docs, or whatever quick way you have taught them to respond with technological tools. Yes, they also can write an "exit slip" on scrap paper and hand it to you as they exit the room.

What usually happens is that students continue reading, anticipating the sentences they copied, and wondering if their inferences have been on or off target. Generally, once they begin, students will keep reading just to validate or expand their thinking.

Decide When Quizzing Is Right

To quiz or not to quiz. We've offered numerous methods you can use to evaluate and assess your students' learning in the context of the daily classroom; however, if your department requires you to include a minimum number of quizzes, here are some points to consider. Quizzes are short measurements of discrete skills. What are you quizzing for? Is it basic understanding of plot or of vocabulary? Will quizzes be scheduled or surprise "pop quizzes"? When giving a quiz, consider making them open book. One idea is to give students the option for their grade. Students can earn up to an "A" using no book; the maximum of a "B" with the book. Quizzes should not be "gotcha" moments.

Consider Links between Cultures and Colors

When the whole class starts a new print book, direct students to bring their books to class. Invite them to look carefully at the front cover first, then at the back cover. Set your timer to ring after seventy-five seconds. Then have students turn toward and talk to partners about what they think the book will be about, just based on the cover graphics: images, colors, and font.

Allot time for a mini lesson in marketing and cover design. Often, publishers change the designs of their covers when issuing new editions, so take a minute and compare book covers. Are there any that are different? If so, have students discuss what changes were made and brainstorm possible reasons why.

Point out that colors have both positive and negative connotations, which vary among cultures. For example, red may mean warm love or cool hate; blue may mean loyalty or sickness; white in Western cultures usually means virginal purity, while in some Eastern cultures it's the color for death, worn by widows. Black in some cultures is worn by adult men to show power; in other cultures, black is reserved for preschool boys to show they have no power . . . yet.

You could just project a slide or distribute a handout, or have learners go to a link on their phones or tablets to quickly explore some of the meanings of assorted colors. Before moving on, ask students what surprised them about what they learned as they explored the different implications of colors and design.

Once they've previewed the book covers or jackets and made their predictions, it's time to flip the books open and look at the pages inside.

Use Color, Shapes, and Arrangement to Show Understanding

Another strategy you will see suggested in the chapters to come involves the use of colors and art. Students can demonstrate their understanding of character motivations, interactions, and relationships through color, shape, and arrangement as well as by sketching and diagramming.

About halfway through the book, assign something that offers creative options where your learners can draw, chart, or diagram what they have been reading, and then share the results with a small group. Yes, this also serves as an assessment tool, and it probably will be evident that some are ahead or behind the assigned reading. Most will finish the assigned reading on time.

If students have access to technology, you could have them use emojis to show the tone used and emotions expressed by the author and the mood and emotions experienced by the reader.

Clarify Writing about Readings

Students usually write well when they know what is expected. The challenge is to resist making the assignment so specific that there is little room for creativity on their part. For this reason, it is helpful to demonstrate that writing is a process during which students discover what they want to say and then, under teacher guidance and with peer feedback, learn how to say it better.

Since you, the instructor, have very definite skills you are asked to teach and must guide the students toward learning them and showing what they know about good writing, it may be useful to work backward by asking yourself questions like these:

1. What skills am I trying to develop or measure in this assignment? Is it how well students understand the text we studied together, how well they can show what they know about analyzing a character, or how well they can write?
2. What will I need to see in students' writing in order to measure their level of understanding or skill? Is it a reference to the text? Is it the use of literary language or rhetorical devices? Is it organization, development of ideas, correct use of vocabulary, grammar, and citations?

If it is all of these, plan a step-by-step lesson in which students do the following:

1. Review the literary language you have been teaching (direct or indirect characterization, motivation, elements of fiction, or adjectives that describe rhetorical devices; compare and contrast; classifying and dividing; explaining a process; narrating) or whatever students are expected to know at this point in the course.
2. Ask students to work together and go back to the text, collaborating to find examples of each of the devices and terms, which they then save in their notes. Allow them to talk together and share their writing. As you listen to their discussions, you gain insight into what they know, empowering you to understand what you need to reteach. If you are working in a virtual setting, set up chat rooms in which small groups of

students can meet and are required to report back to the whole group. Plan time for the whole-group sharing.

3. Invite students to write a statement of their opinion about the topic you assign and have them use a modifier (adjective or adverb word, phrase, or clause) to indicate their thinking about
   - how well or poorly they think the author develops the characters,
   - how much they identify with the characters or personages,
   - to what extent they agree or disagree with the stance the author takes on the topic of the fiction or nonfiction text, and
   - how they see connections to everyday incidents in the way one or more characters act or react in the story or situation in the text.

In their essays, students will then attempt to show why their modifier is true or valid.

At this point your learners can begin writing "PIE" paragraphs, in which they state their *position* or opinion; *illustrate with examples* from the beginning, middle, and end of the text; and then, *explain* ways those references support their position or opinion. Explaining is the most important element because it shows your learners' level of understanding.

The students should be ready to write an introduction paragraph to lead into their body paragraph(s) and a conclusion paragraph to reflect on or summarize what they have written, without introducing new ideas. Knowing there are no wrong answers, only unsupported ones, frees students to write eagerly and honestly. Consider using the following methods:

1. Rather than show students a fully polished sample essay, write along with them, demonstrating how you build your essay.
2. Invite students to do an internet search for words to describe writing or use the ones mentioned in chapter 6, based on the recommendations of Jim Burke.
3. Project your grading rubric, which includes the minimum traits you expect to see in terms of content, organization, and correctness.
4. Ask the students to reflect on their drafts, share them with partners to get feedback, revise them, and then submit the papers for you to evaluate, using the same rubric you provide when you give each assignment.

Yes, this is a little formulaic, but it works well for less-confident students to write about their reading in this kind of essay. It also confirms for confident writers that they are on the right road to success in your course. Many eventually choose a pattern they like better that shows equally well what you need to see to assess their learning. This process results in empowered learning and learners.

BUILDING IN LESSONS FOR WRITING
IN DIFFERENT GENRES

Think about sports, music, and art. Who seems to appreciate a baseball game, an opera, or an unusual piece of abstract art? Usually, it is a current or former athlete, musician, or artist, respectively. They know firsthand the skill and discipline it takes to play the game, make the music, or create the art. You can inspire respect for diverse authors by designing lessons for students to draft in various genres. Not only does it offer the opportunity to dive into the genre, but it also gives a welcome break from the traditional essay format. Furthermore, as students experience writing in different categories, their level of understanding and enjoyment may even make them fans.

No, you do not have to make yours a traditional creative-writing class, but you can include assignments where students sample both reading and writing. For example, for a homework assignment, you could have students copy from their text into their journals three different sentences that help readers to visualize a person, a place, or an incident. Then, during class, as students share their sentences, talk about ways syntax and vocabulary create images in the minds of readers. Afterward, have the students follow the pattern of their favorite sentences but write about something they have experienced, observed, or learned about in another course.

After studying short stories, you might assign students to draft or outline one; do the same for poetry and drama. It might not be an entire short story or play, but perhaps a vignette or an act. Once they have read, written, and talked about different categories of text and have also tried writing them, they will have a deeper appreciation for authors who write so well in those engaging genres.

Some students may even decide to enter writing contests offered at your college or university or by local and state libraries. Consider national contests like the Rattle Poetry Prize, Wells Festival of Literature's Competitions, University of New Orleans Press Publishing Lab Prize, and the HG Wells Short Story Competition.

MANAGING GRADING WITH GENERAL
GRADING GUIDELINES

While all the reading, talking, using art, and writing is going on, you also have the responsibility to conduct assessments, not only to measure student learning but also to gauge your own teaching. Students, administrators, and paying parents want to know how you determine growth in your learners. The

GENERAL GRADING GUIDELINES

A = complete, correct, and creative
B = complete and correct
C = complete
D = deficient
F = failing, for now

C = THE SEA – Complete (includes all components of the assignment)
B = THE BOAT – Complete and **Correct** (rides on the sea with minimal errors in mechanics, usage, grammar, and spelling)
A = THE SAIL – Complete, Correct, and **Creative** *(something above and beyond the boat; original and fresh elements enhancing final performance/product)*

Share grading guidelines with students and administrators.

Anna Created Graphic with Boat https://www.istockphoto.com/vector/sailboat-in-the-sea-concept-for-the -tourist-company-gm817695182-132322351

sooner you decide how to communicate this, the more efficiently you will be able to construct lessons that reveal what you need to know and what students need to show that they are making progress under your instruction.

Assessment involves measuring where students are and how much they have learned. Evaluation requires placing a value on that growth and, most often, assigning a grade. Determining grades is the bane of most instructors, but using a grading rubric helps in this often-difficult process. Rubrics can be designed for individual assignments, units, or the entire semester. By establishing a rubric, the teacher will be able to clearly determine a final grade. Likewise, because clear expectations have been given at the beginning of the assignment or semester, students will be able to determine how well they are doing throughout the class.

Keep reading to see a more detailed discussion of rubrics. The diagram above shows that to earn a "C" on a process assignment (one on which students have time to get feedback and do revising), the document, product, or performance must be *complete*; it must include the basic components of the assignment. To earn a "B," the product or performance should be *complete and correct*; it must have few distracting errors in mechanics, usage, grammar, or spelling (MUGS) for writing, and sloppiness for performances. To earn an "A," the writing, artwork, or oral or video performance should be *complete, correct, and creative*, reflecting freshness in language, originality that is unexpected but effective, and revealing qualities that can only be acknowledged as something over and above completeness and correctness.

Customize Rubrics

A rubric, according to Heidi Andrade's commonly accepted definition, is a chart to assess a document, product, or performance. The chart articulates the expectations for an assignment by listing the criteria, or what counts, and describing levels of quality from excellent to poor. If your school or department does not have a general rubric for your course, consider the Six Traits for Writing©. The more recent version, Six Traits Plus One, has the following seven traits:

- ideas—the main message
- organization—the internal structure of the piece
- voice—the personal tone and flavor of the writer's message
- word choice—the vocabulary a writer chooses to convey meaning
- sentence fluency—the rhythm and flow of the language
- conventions—the mechanical correctness
- presentation—effective use of oral and visual elements and media

Share this rubric with the class early in the course and then customize it for subsequent assignments, adding the specific elements or content learned since and expected on that assignment. For example, for *ideas/content* after having studied various literary devices, you may customize the assignment to say that, to be complete, the student work must include examples from the reading that show three-to-five literary devices. Or, to be complete, the student must quote or reference examples from the beginning, middle, and end of the reading or from three different reliable online sources. For more experienced students, you may require your learners to quote from critical analyses of the work about which the students are writing.

After teaching, modeling, and practicing a particular grammatical structure or style of referencing citations, you may customize the rubric's *sentence fluency* trait to indicate that, to be complete and correct, the student work must include four different sentence starts. The *conventions* section could state that citations must be in Chicago style (or whatever style your school or college department uses).

Customizing rubrics serves multiple purposes that empower you, the teacher, as well as the range of student learners in your class. When you are preparing the assignment, you know what you need to see to measure learning, so include that on the rubric. Even more critical, the customized rubric helps you align your testing with your teaching without teaching to the test.

Gradually Increase the Weight of Assignments

At the start of the course, big assignments (process papers, projects, and presentations, for which students have time to plan, get peer feedback, and revise) need not be weighted heavily enough to "kill" a quarterly grade. Similar high standards can be given for each assignment, but students have time to see the standards and get feedback on their performance and seldom are so discouraged that they stop trying. It might be helpful to weight the assignments ahead of time, deciding which are more important, but ultimately when added together equal one-hundred percent.

Let Students Conduct Self-Grading.

We are big fans of self-grading. No, you will not be giving up control when you invite students to use the general grading guidelines and customized rubric to tell you what they think they earned. Instead, you are inviting them to reflect on their work and point out how their document, product, or performance demonstrates the grade they say they sought. They already have the rubric that you will use in evaluating the assignment. Your goal has been for them to reference that rubric throughout, so it only makes sense for them to use it to judge their own final work. The challenge for you will be to resist looking at their grades before you complete your evaluations.

Have students send an email or staple a folded note to their assignment. Hold on to these until you have completed the grading. Another idea is to provide students with a print copy of the rubric that you will be using. Have students submit that rubric sheet the day their assignment is due. You will be using the front, but have the students write on the back of the rubric the grade they assigned themselves and three specific ways their paper, product, or performance has earned that grade.

After you have completed the grading for a paper, check what the student has said. Then, if the student's grade matches yours, raise that grade one half-step. A "C+" becomes a "B-"; a "B-" becomes a "B"; a "B" becomes a "B+"; a "B+" becomes an "A." It only takes three or four "rounds" at most before students begin grading themselves correctly. Usually, it happens more quickly. Seldom will students over-reward themselves. More often they will assign themselves a lower grade. No need, however, to change a grade if a student grades him or herself lower; the comments on the grading sheet will show your reasoning for the higher grade. Learners will be pleased, and fewer students or administrators will challenge your grading. Students will gain confidence in their own writing, presentation, and media making. You will be pleased.

Plan to Be Firm, Fair, and Flexible

No matter how carefully educators plan, something unexpected comes up in their students' lives, something that calls for acts of mercy. You can avoid seeming rigid with deadlines if you build in a safety net that does not increase the workload for you. One that has worked for many veteran educators is a *one-time-use late pass*.

During the first week of the course, but not on the first day, give students a printed or numerical late pass they can use *once* during the course. This pass can be used to turn in the final document or product one class period late without losing credit. If the pass is not used, the late coupon can be turned in for credit before its expiration date one week before the marking period ends. The credit can be ten points or whatever the late penalty would have been.

The value of this late-pass policy is that its use need not disrupt your teaching and grading. Few teachers can grade all final documents (written papers) or products (art or media projects) in just a few days, so having one come in late usually does not extend the grading time as much as receiving one poorly done. Having students earn an extra ten points during a marking period will probably just make up for a low quiz grade earned when the student was unprepared.

Oral presentations, however, are scheduled during class time, and giving an oral presentation late could be disruptive to the class schedule. For that reason, it may not be wise to permit the use of a late pass for late presentations. If, on the other hand, the presentation is electronic and you and students can view it at another time, that assignment may be eligible for late-pass credit. You decide what would be fair and not create more work for you.

Consider Full Credit for On-Time
Preliminary Assignments

Plan grading that assigns full credit for on-time early steps and gives students fewer reasons to get too far behind. For example, on a multiple-step assignment leading to a heavily weighted document, project, or performance, you might weight a one-hundred-point assignment in the following way:

- Ten points for a written plan or outline that is submitted on time
- Fifteen points for an on-time first draft
- Fifteen points for written courteous, constructive feedback that is provided to peers and completed on time
- Up to fifty points for an on-time final document, product, or performance (based on the grading rubric)
- Ten points for an on-time self-reflection and grading

Or, if specific rhetorical features are being focused on, you might want to further break down the fifty points reserved for the final document. You might subdivide the points among the introduction, the use of examples, the strength of the conclusion, the mechanics, and other elements. If your focus that week was on using engaging introductions, then that might be something to consider. Additionally, if the assignment includes a creative twist, you might consider allowing ten points for miscellaneous style or author voice—the wow factor. Regardless of how you break it out, the bulk of the grade should reflect the overall success of the final draft, and the students should know ahead of time exactly how and on what their writing will be evaluated.

Considering the time and purpose of grading will help you adapt this approach to fit the assignments you design and the college population you teach. Keep in mind that building in flexibility makes it less stressful to be firm, and you will be viewed as a fair teacher who understands the reality of being a student. More importantly, you will reduce the stress on students. Most importantly, you and your students will remain on the road to success with your teaching and their learning.

METHODICAL ENDING

Plan to end each class meeting in an orderly fashion by having a timer alert you when five minutes remain. Use that time for reflection and projection.

Reflection

Consider using an exit-slip strategy that invites students to summarize or question what they learned during the current class meeting. If technology is easily accessible, have students send the exit slip to your learning platform (i.e., Moodle, Blackboard, Google Classroom, or to your dedicated email). Alternatively, students may write the exit slip on scrap paper and hand it to you as they leave. For the sake of time, ask for just a sentence or two.

You may project sentence stems like these or others you find online that better fit your setting:

- Today I learned . . .
- I better understand . . .
- I don't understand . . .
- I'd like to learn more about . . .

Projection

Next, announce and briefly explain the homework due on or before the next class meeting. Show the students where on the website or assignment sheet they can find specifics about the work they are to complete. Do they bring it to class or upload their work on the learning platform? Consider including in your announcement the reason why you are assigning the homework. Students will do (or at least try to do) almost anything for you if they understand *why* you're asking them to do it and *how* it will help them. You may explain that the homework is designed for learners to

- practice strategy(ies) or skill(s) presented in the current or in a past class meeting
- prepare for the next class meeting (read, write, research, collaborate)
- polish a paper or product for presentation online or in class
- ponder plans for upcoming assignment or performance on recent assignment.

Versions of this orderly ending of class meetings should continue throughout the course. Even if you have experienced students, your taking time to reflect on the current class meeting and explain upcoming assignments, showing where to find the specifics and verbalizing rationales for assignments, benefits both you and the students.

You, the teacher, will have considered the value of the assignment and ways it will help students learn or demonstrate what they are learning. Students will feel empowered because they will not have to worry about locating what is required and can ask questions before they leave class.

CONCLUSION

Now that you have contemplated ways to lay the groundwork, strap on your seatbelts and get ready for the ride. It won't always be smooth. There will be bumps and potholes. There may be construction and you'll need to reroute.

Learning to navigate the journey and successfully arriving at your destination is the goal. Along the way, as you continue reading and referring to sections in the chapters that follow, you will have time to refuel your tanks with more ideas for the following:

- teaching vocabulary for reading
- managing grades
- assessing understanding informally and formally
- writing about and in response to reading
- using a variety of means to show understanding
- planning homework that is strategically designed for students to practice, prepare, polish, or ponder what they are learning
- accessing supplemental materials from in-person and online sources

You've been hired to design and deliver learning experiences that teach the different genres generally taught in basic English language arts courses to learners of different ages, prior experiences, cultures, and languages. Keep reading to add to your tank the knowledge, insight, energy, and inspiration for the miles to come.

Chapter Three

Networking with Narratives to Create Community

"Getting to know you, getting to know all about you. Getting to like you, getting to hope you like me."[1]

–Oscar Hammerstein, *The King and I*

Even in the age of electronic social networking, in-person relationships are the most meaningful for teachers and learners. The classroom itself is a "site" for social networking among increasingly diverse students, first-year classroom instructors, graduate-student instructors, student assistants (GTA/GSIs), two-year college instructors, and adjunct professors. To prepare for learning on this journey, it is essential to prime the pump, increase the flow of ideas, and ready students to work together to explore, explain, and express themselves in multiple oral and written formats. Reading often is the fuel to empower learning to write. The Council of Writing Program Administrators (WPA) says in its course outcome goals that, by the end of the first year, college students should be able to

- participate effectively in collaborative processes and
- review work in progress for the purpose of developing ideas before doing surface-level editing.[2]

Reading model texts, telling stories, and writing narratives are effective and efficient ways to begin meeting these course goals.

You may have planned a couple of ice-breaker activities for the first day to help you and your students get to know one another and you. Now, how about considering a narrative-writing assignment based on names to discover your students' current writing agility and to assess how nimble they are at reading and conducting research? This sample lesson includes options that permit you

35

to informally assess skills your students bring to class, whether you are teaching basic composition, introductory science, math, or social studies.

EXPLORE AND WRITE ABOUT NAMES

According to Ralph Ellison:

> We must wear our names within all the noise and confusion of the environment in which we find ourselves; make them the center of all our associations with the world, with man and with nature. We must charge them with all our emotions, our hopes, hates, loves, aspirations. They must become our masks and our shields, and the containers of all those values and traditions which we learn and/ or imagine as being the meaning of our familial past.[3]

Names are important. They can distinguish one thing from another and link a person to families, cultures, and communities. Names can make students proud or embarrassed, one with others, and separate from others. This paradox of emotions that names can produce poses a challenge and an opportunity. This enigma makes for an intriguing way to communicate culture and identity with lessons that can help establish a community of supportive learners who know about one another and become willing to share their writing and exchange feedback with classmates.

Depending on your college or university, students in your class may be away from home for the first time or attending college where they know no one else. Many are freshmen, eager to become independent of their parents or guardians, often straining against the ties that bind them. These young adults are developing their self-identities distinct from those of their families. Joining your young students may be those taking their first college classes as adults, and as nontraditional students they may be considerably older than some of their classmates. Writing about names can help bridge this gap and build a trusting learning community in a nonthreatening way. Perhaps it is because the students will be doing what so many like to do best—talking about themselves!

Remaining Alert: Words of Caution

Writing about names, however, may evoke trigger moments, causing emotional difficulties for some students. So, be sensitive to the fact that some may resist this project for reasons related to personal trauma. Be prepared to adapt rather than scrap this getting-to-know-you assignment. Students quite often prefer using abbreviated names or nicknames rather than the formal or legal name listed on your class list. While formally taking roll during the first class, ask for correct pronunciation of names and then note phonetically or otherwise for your future reference. At this time you can also ask for a preferred name and note that as well. For example, Geoffrey Michael may wish to go by Mike. Regardless, make every effort to learn the names of your students and use those preferred names when addressing them.

Learning someone's name is one of the highest forms of respect. The activities that follow as well as other ice-breaker activities help students learn more about their classmates. Share the reason why you are doing the activity. Make explicit to them the importance of learning each other's names and how that builds trust and fosters the sense of community that is critical to learning.

Considering Ethnicities

Discussing the issue of names and ancestry proves to be difficult for some students and impossible for others. Prior to the 1860s, the birth records of African Americans included few surnames and, when kept at all, first names often were recorded among the cattle records. Even in the twenty-first century, few African Americans can trace their ancestry more than a few generations. Those families who can trace their history may already know that they carry the surnames of slave owners. Most know that their families originated

Get to know them—write away.
https://www.istockphoto.com/photo/college-students-with-books-smiling-to-camera-over-grey-wall
　-gm1167992655-322324937

on the continent of Africa, but,few have access to information that can verify the country or the tribe.

Families of new-to-America students may have come to escape political unrest in their country of origin. Some students may be able but unwilling to discuss their names. Ancestors may have changed their names as protection against political repercussions. On the other hand, such students may appreciate the fact that you are interested in learning more about their culture and are thrilled with the opportunity to talk about it.

A teacher who is new to the campus or community knows to confer with veteran educators at the college and then adapt the lessons as needed to gain the benefits and avoid the pitfalls. The more diverse your school's community, the more careful you need to be. Consider adapting the assignment so the writings can be based on real or imagined incidents. Remember, in addition to getting to know each other, this first writing exercise also allows you to assess current writing abilities.

With so many pitfalls, why bother? Because just reading texts about naming and living with names can be a rich, intellectual experience for your students.

In addition, the accompanying assignments help meet several course outcome goals in interesting and illuminating ways as you design lessons for

- reading, discussing, and analyzing texts in a variety of genres;
- learning content-specific vocabulary;
- conducting various kinds of research (online, library, and interview);
- writing brief autobiographical sketches for a narrative assignment;
- participating in peer editing groups; and
- giving oral reports.

Select Literary Works about Names

One way to begin is with a lesson you can simply call "What's in a Name?," based on Sandra Cisneros's autobiographical vignette about growing up as a child of Mexican immigrants in Chicago.[4] You may have done a similar assignment yourself and recall how much you learned about your own family and those of your classmates. Follow up with "Hidden Name and Complex Fate," an essay by Ralph Ellison, an African American named by his father for Ralph Waldo Emerson, the renowned White American poet. The Ellison essay works incredibly well as a springboard for writing stories based on experiences in living with one's names. A more complete explanation of the lesson is found later in the chapter.

Read "Hidden Name and Complex Fate" to see how students handle nonfiction essay texts. Point out that expository writing uses text structures your learners may have learned in high school. Students may even recall the terms: description, sequence, cause and effect, compare and contrast, and problem and solution. If necessary, find and show an online video as a mini lesson to review these structures with your students. Ellison's essay inspired the questions you can use for the students' research and writing about their own names (see box titled "RESEARCH and WRITE about YOUR NAMES" later in this chapter).

Have students begin reading during the class. Doing so gives you an opportunity to informally assess students' approaches to different genres. This knowledge will help you design future lessons based on the skill levels of the students in your class. One of the WPA outcome goals relates to reading analytically and critically. Start now to determine which skills your students have and those for which you may need to design lessons to help them learn.

Read, Research, and Learn the Vocabulary of Names

As an educator, you know the value of reading and analyzing model texts to discover their effectiveness. Paying attention to organizational patterns, diction, and sentence structure helps readers focus on reasons the writing works for the purpose intended. For this assignment, you may want to introduce content-specific vocabulary of naming: surname, given name, nickname, nom de plume, pseudonym, pen name, and alias.

Encourage students to interview a family member to gather information about how and why the students have come to have the names they carry. You may need to review with your student researchers the correct way to cite an interview in the text of the essay and to format their bibliographies based on the style used at your college.

With expanded resources available on the internet, most students are able to find enough information to fulfill the basic purposes of the assignment— to consider their own names, conduct research, and write about family or cultural traditions of naming that they discover. If students have uncommon names or common names that are spelled uncommonly, they may need a bit of help identifying similar, researchable alternatives. Prepare them by showing them different spellings of the same name, such as Anna, Ana, Ann, Anne, Annie, Anouska, Anya, and even Hannah.

Students might benefit from using ancestry.com and similar websites to collect historical information about their family names. By all means, share your name story and write along with your students. We shouldn't ask our students to do anything we're not willing to do ourselves.

As students consider responses to these prompts, they reflect on who they are in their families, the college, the wider community, and perhaps even the world. Some students may learn family history that was never previously discussed. Others awaken tender memories of relatives and family friends for whom they have been named. Some may be sadly embarrassed, others pleasantly surprised.

Discover Interesting Cultural Information about Naming

This research assignment is a good one to introduce students to one of several ways to give and receive courteous and constructive feedback. As students read about name-related experiences during peer-response sessions, they discover surprising naming traditions observed in the families of their classmates. They might learn that, in some villages in India, all the girls in a family may have the same middle name; or that some Thai families carry extremely long, polysyllabic names, like Prachyaratanawooti, for which each syllable represents a generation the family has lived in that region. Students might learn that, in some families, it is the grandmother who chooses grandchildren's names, that the eldest son always is named for his father, or that the middle name for all the children is their mother's maiden name.

Your students may notice interesting combinations of Anglo and Asian or Spanish names. Some students find out that their families' names have been Americanized to avoid discrimination based on ethnicity, religion, or nationality. A number of your students may have saints' day names or hyphenated last names that include both their mother's maiden name and their father's last name. Some learn the spelling of their surnames is simply the result of an error made when their ancestors entered the country through Ellis Island in New York or Angel Island in San Francisco. No one ever bothered to correct the mistake.

One of the assignment prompts invites students to talk about the challenges of living with their names, as described in "Hidden Name and Complex Fate." Some student writing may reveal that carrying the name of a particularly famous or infamous relative causes them discomfort. One young man who was named for his father, a prominent businessperson in the community, acknowledged in his essay that he felt unworthy to be called Robert and insisted that his peers call him Robbie, a diminutive version of the father's strong name. Cecilia, a talented singer, was depressed for a few days on learning that the name she loves means "blind one," then was jubilant after discovering that St. Cecilia is the patron saint of music and musicians.

Other students may write about the embarrassment of having to correct the pronunciation of their names at the beginning of every school year and the frustration of having to spell their names everywhere they go. These reminders of sensitivity surrounding names remind us to learn to pronounce and spell each student's name as early in the course as possible. It is just another way of honoring each one as an individual with his or her own special names.

Springboarding to Writing Narratives

Distribute a copy of the vignette "My Name," by Sandra Cisneros, and pre-pare to conduct a "jump-in reading" activity to help students get a feel for Cisneros's style and to think about what the writer may be saying to them. First, ask students to read silently, underlining words or phrases that catch their attention. Then, you read the vignette out loud, asking students again to underline words or phrases they think are interesting or important.

Finally, starting at the beginning again, invite one student to begin reading aloud, stopping at the first mark of punctuation. Invite others to jump in to read, without being called upon, and to read to the next punctuation mark. If more than one student begins reading at the same time, urge each to listen to the other(s) and to read as one voice. Between voices, let the silence resonate.

Students may be uncomfortable at first and giggle a bit, but they will soon catch on. The silence between the sounds of different single voices and com-binations of multiple voices leaves indelible impressions and elicits powerful results in the next step of this assignment.

To help the students get started in composing their narratives, after reading "My Name," ask them to do a "quick write." A quick write means writing for a short period, nonstop, on an assigned topic. For a brief period—three to five minutes—students let their thoughts flow without censoring them. In this assignment, ask students to copy an underlined phrase or sentence from the reading. Instruct them to then use that phrase or sentence as a jumping-off point to write rapidly about their own names. Write along with them. The fol-lowing is a quick write based on Cisneros's piece:

> "My Name," a Quick Write by Anna Jamar Small Roseboro,
> Inspired by Sandra Cisneros's Vignette of the Same Name

Is this "me"? My name is a combination of my paternal grandmother's, Anna; my maternal grandmother's, Jamie; my dad's name, Small; and my husband's name, Roseboro. Everyone has had my name—made something of it, then passed it along to me. Anna means "gift of God." Is it I who am the gift or my grandmother who is a gift to me? Jamie is short for Jamar. My grandmother, whose full name is Jamar Elna, is named after her four aunts, Jane, Martha, Ellen, and Nora—what a burden, what a privilege, to carry the names of so many relatives. Or is it a blessing? Am I standing on the shoulders of those who've come before me?

Small, my maiden name, always caused me trouble. "Small," they'd tease. "You're not small; you're tall!" I was always the tallest girl in my elementary school classes. In high school, however, I used the name to my advantage. I ran for a senior class office. My slogan was, "Good things come in Small packages." Finally, success with that name.

Then, I married Bill Roseboro during the years that Johnny Roseboro was a star catcher for the L. A. Dodgers. He'd been in the news because of a fight with Juan Marichal. Everywhere I went, "Are you related to Johnny Roseboro?" "Yes, but what has that to do with me?" Who am I really?

RESEARCH AND WRITE ABOUT YOUR NAMES

- Use a dictionary and/or online resources to find out what each of your own names *means*.
- Interview a family member to learn the *sources* of your name(s). Consider recording or videotaping the interview.
- Who *named you* and why? Are you named for a friend or family member? Someone else?
- Determine the *kind of surname* or last name you have. Is it a place name, like Al-Fassi, Hall, or Rivera; an occupation, like Chandler, Smith, or Taylor; a descriptive, Braun or Strong; or a patronymic or version of a father's name, like Ben-Yehuda, McNeil, or Von Wilhelm?
- Describe incidents you have *experienced* because of your name, including mispronunciations, misspellings, and misunderstandings.
- Write about *nicknames* and related embarrassing or humorous experiences.
- Identify *challenges* you feel because of the name(s) you carry.

Extending the Experience or Keeping It Brief

Yes, it is worth allotting dedicated class time for an assignment like this because it is a useful, efficient way to do four things that are important to success in any course:

- Get to know the students
- Introduce or review basic writing-process concepts: prewriting, drafting, and giving and receiving feedback before revising
- Discover students' prior knowledge, academic vocabulary, and writing strategies they already know
- Provide an opening assignment that most will find interesting to complete

One professor made this "Living with a Name" activity an interview assignment during which students, working in pairs, interviewed one another. They next wrote about what they had learned, then introduced their partner to the class, using what they had learned in the interview. Assignments that start with students talking and writing about themselves in ways that are comfortable to them and informative to their classmates help create a community of learners.

If you decide to extend this unit beyond the first few class meetings, consider substituting or reading a chapter from Richard E. Kim's *Lost Names: Scenes from a Korean Boyhood*, about Korean families forced by the government of Japan to adopt Japanese names; *Not Even My Name*, an autobiographical work by Thea Halo about Pontic Greeks in Turkey; or *The Namesake*, a novel by Jhumpa Lahiri, about the naming traditions of a family from India.[5]

Let your own interests and the cultures and interests of your students guide your selections each time. As always, select readings to fit your current setting, texts that serve as windows for seeing others and as mirrors for seeing oneself. Consider inviting students to write about the names of key figures in your content areas, like Einstein for science and math; James Lipton in the arts; Alan Turing in technology; Dolores Huerta or John Lewis for history. To keep this personal, encourage students to research and write about someone with a name that begins with the same letter as the student's first or last name.

GIVING AND RECEIVING PEER FEEDBACK

The goals of most first-year composition courses include having students know when, why, and how to give and receive courteous, constructive feedback. Having instructors who are also the guide from the side can be more valuable than their being only the sage from the stage. In other words, design lessons for which students learn to do more for one another instead of depending only on you.

In this book are several ways to frame lessons and organize the class sessions during which students give and receive peer feedback, ways that lead to meaningful revision. The challenge, however, may be motivating students to revise. Jessica Hudson, when she was a graduate teaching assistant, shared that the "issue with teaching revision [is a] lack of motivation. For many students, it seems once it's written, it's written. They're not interested in seeing how it could be improved because they don't see the worth in it already!" Often, students' resistance to revision comes from the fact that they don't know how to revise.

Students may proofread and edit for spelling and punctuation, but they also need to learn about the crafting of writing. Revision means "to see again," and students need to experience rewriting their piece and recognizing how that "revision" improves it. Their lack of motivation comes from not seeing the benefit of improving their writing when the teacher is the sole audience. Shifting their audience from the teacher to their classmates often provides the motivation they need. Of course they want to impress their peers, and the feedback from them will be taken seriously. Motivation seldom is a problem when students are writing about themselves. As you foster a safe community of writers, students learn how to communicate in supportive ways that challenge themselves and their peers to improve their composition and communication skills. The following exercise helps do both.

Starting with a Read-Around Group Session

A read-around group (RAG) session for giving and receiving peer feedback works well at the start of most courses. This is sometimes referred to as a writer's workshop. Students bring to the class a printed draft of their name essay. You provide a simple version of your grading rubric. (See sample in chapter 1.) Arrange circles of five or six students. Once students have settled, you review with them the rubric, noting the traits on which the final narrative essay will be evaluated. This rubric, a chart with numbers (1–5) for rating the traits, will guide students' reading and commenting about the drafts of their peers.

While most students will have devices on which to work electronically, consider doing this first RAG activity with pens and paper. Once students are comfortable with the process, they can transfer that knowledge to their work on electronic platforms. For now, focus on the *what* and *why* of this work for them and for you. The *what* for them is to give and receive feedback and learn how to workshop their own writing. The *what* for you is to see how your new students handle this step in the process. The *why* for them is to see what classmates are writing and to learn what the writers can do better as they revise before submitting their stories for assessment/grading. The *why* for you is to get better-written narratives that won't take so long to read and grade.

For this first RAG experience,

- have students write their names on the rubric and lay it on top of their drafts;
- have one student from each group collect all the drafts and hand them to you;
- you distribute the drafts to other groups so that no one is reading the paper of anyone else in their group (group A gets group B papers, group

B gets group C papers, etc.—this way, students are less likely to be distracted by watching how classmates respond to their paper); and,
- during the RAG session, each student reads five or six papers but responds to only two.

Do not allow those without a draft to sit in on a RAG session. Fairness suggests that paperless students sit out and use the time to work. First, it is useful to give those who are behind class time to catch up. Second, if a student in a group does not have a paper to be read during each round, then someone else has to "sit out" because of too few papers. Since on-time submission of the first draft is a graded component of the process, there is no need to worry about students coming unprepared the next time. Most are ready for the next RAG session because they want to see what others have written and they also want to get feedback and suggestions for their own revisions. Curiosity is a great motivator.

Once the groups are formed and have their stack of papers, the group leader distributes the drafts to group members, and you set a timer for three to four minutes, which usually is enough time to read the two or three pages of these early drafts. Students read the first paper until the timer goes off, then pass the paper to the right and read the second paper, the third paper, and the fourth paper until the timer goes off again. After the fourth pass, set the timer for six minutes.

Next, the students read and comment on the content of the paper. On the fifth pass, again set the timer for six minutes; the students read and comment on the organization and style.

Then, students write one sentence of commendation and one sentence with a recommendation for that classmate to consider during revision.

By this time, the students have learned

- a great deal about their classmates;
- ways their peers have responded to the prompts;
- problems that arise when one makes mechanical, usage, grammar, and spelling errors; and, equally enlightening,
- the quality of the pool of writing in which their own papers are to be read.

While students are reading the first two or three drafts, you can walk around the classroom and record in your grade book a check for the students who have their drafts ready on this due date. Afterward, during the longer reading times, you have a few moments to confer with those who have come unprepared; offer suggestions to get them back on track with their writing.

At the end of the RAG session, each leader collects the group's papers and hands them to you.

Before returning the papers and rubrics to the students who wrote them, spend five or six minutes soliciting from the class the strengths—using terms from the rubric—they noticed in the papers and inviting suggested strategies for improving the strengths. There is no need to mention weaknesses at this time.

If you are in a setting where students write only electronically, adapt this assignment so that students still read several drafts before writing comments.

- Have students upload their assignments in a folder you have set up on the class learning platform (Blackboard, Google Classroom, Moodle, or whatever).
- Then, before the class meets, create subfolders into which you drag and drop five or six student drafts in alphabetical order by last name.
- Label those folders A through D or E (depending on your class size). Then create a class list arranged in alphabetical order by last name.
- Assign each student a letter and a number. The letter is for the folder the student is to read and respond to, and the number will be used to locate the specific student drafts that the student is to respond to.
- Create a list that shows students are assigned to a folder that *does not* contain their draft. Since the folders include drafts in alphabetical order, this assignment should not be time-consuming for you.
- Then, when students get to the *responding* step in the RAG process, show another slide with this reading instruction: "Using your assigned number, begin reading the draft with that number, and read the next draft in order. Students #1 responds to drafts 2 and 3. Students #3 comments on drafts 4 and 5. Student #5 comments on drafts 1 and 2."
- Comment on *content* for that first assigned draft and *organization* on that second assigned draft. With a chart showing, students can handle this.
  - Allow ten to twelve minutes to read as much as they can of drafts 1 through 5. Having a timer buzz every two to three minutes helps keep them on track.
  - Then set a timer for
    - seven to nine minutes to read and comment on *content* of draft 1 and
    - six to eight minutes to read and comment on *organization* of draft 2.

Be alert to timing so that there is an opportunity before class ends for students to see where to find the comments about their drafts. Allot the final ten minutes of class meeting for an orderly closing of the RAG session.

Responding after a Read-Around Group
Session: Before Class Time Ends

Return the papers to the writers or show them the folders with their drafts. Direct them to read the comments from their peers and then to write three steps they will take as writers to revise their written narrative. Have the timer ring five minutes before the end of the period so you can summarize the experience and give the homework assignment.

Consider using "Flip!" (formerly, "FLIP-GRID") as an option for students to give oral feedback to their peers in virtual settings or for subsequent home-work assignments. Students can be assigned to email their revision plan to you within twenty-four hours. This email creates a record that the students have received feedback and have outlined a plan for revising. These stated plans can be a starting point when you begin reading the final papers and note whether the writers implemented their plans.

Assign the students to have their final drafts ready for you after two class meetings. During the intervening days, schedule in-class writing time for students to work on their revisions. If your students meet just once a week, do this RAG assignment during the second segment of the class meeting; then, after their break, have students begin revising during the final segment of the class.

Do not feel frustrated if you find yourself adjusting the length of time needed for revision. Ask the students. Thankfully, students become person-ally invested in these papers and want you to see their best work. Do both them and yourself a favor—create a schedule that is flexible enough to allow them to revise. Well-written papers are a pleasure to read and take less time to grade.

If you teach in a setting where it is unrealistic to expect students to word-process the final drafts at home, provide additional class time for students to use school equipment. Especially in writing, it is important that students complete a few assignments well rather than rush through many assignments that they cannot finish carefully and turn in with pride. This name-writing narrative is one to which they usually are willing to devote time. The subjects, after all, are the students themselves.

On the due date, for evaluation, students should submit a packet or upload a folder that includes their first drafts, the rubric with their plan, and the final copy (on the top of other documents in the packet or at the top of the list of documents in the folder). This stack of papers or this folder of documents substantiates that the process of writing is a lot of work. If students have worked completely online and have done online peer reviews instead of RAG sessions, then students should save and submit all numbered drafts in their student folders, which you can view online. See subsequent chapters for different configurations for online peer-response sessions.

Considering a Human-Interest Story

Another engaging way to invite students to write narratives or articles is based on their content major or the special license or certification they seek to earn in college. The prompt is simple, and responding to it can include the student doing some basic research, leading to the student composing a newspaper article describing an imaginary event during which the student is honored by members of their profession. The writing prompt is "With what prestigious award will you be honored in ten or fifteen years?" Student essays should include the following:

- Introduction: who, what, when, where, why, and how about the award ceremony
- Body paragraphs:
  - Education and career of the winner (the student by the time of the award)
  - Others who have won the honor in the past
  - Ways this year's winner (the student) compares to former winners

Reading student writing reveals how you're teaching.

https://www.istockphoto.com/photo/head-shot-serious-puzzled-african-american-businessman-looking-at-laptop-gm1156269818-315068330

- Conclusion: when and where the award will be given next year
- A photo: after revising and editing their article, the students should add a recent photo of themselves (it should be uploaded to the student's online folder on the class learning platform)

Respecting the Writing Process

These steps in the process of drafting a paper are important for new college classroom teachers, individual writers, and their classmates. Scheduling this assignment early in the course allows you to observe how students handle various steps in the writing process. You can expect them to be able to take these steps with relative independence by the second half of the term. Based on what you observe in the opening two or three weeks, you can design or adapt lessons that are appropriate for students in each of your classes.

As the students exchange feedback during the interim stages of writing, they see how peers are addressing the assignment. For many students, this is both a comfort and a challenge. When they see that they and their peers are having similar problems, they do not feel so odd or incompetent. On the other hand, when they see how well some of their peers are doing, individual students realize that the task is possible, and they are challenged to work a little harder to meet the assignment standards.

Building on Prior Knowledge

Your students may be new to college but are not new travelers along the road of life. They are joining you for just this portion of a lifelong journey of living and learning. As a new college instructor or GTA/GSI, you are both a fellow traveler and tour guide.

You have the responsibility to do all you can to prepare students for the weeks and months ahead, perhaps warning them of possible landslides that can occur or inclement weather they may experience, always assuring them that you are in this together. You are there to help them climb the rock walls of new tasks that seem unscalable; to work with them, eager to observe them open their hearts and minds to see and appreciate the beauty of reading, writing, and discussing culturally relevant issues and employing ethical use of rhetorical devices.

You will help them think about new kinds of writing, novel narratives, and fascinating essays, readying them to explore natural wonders encountered along the way. Most of all, you will guide their practice and use of skills as they strive to achieve their personal goals, achieving success in any content area or field of study.

CONCLUSION

Seriously consider using a narrative-writing unit as an efficient way to blend reading and writing, helping establish a nurturing environment in which students can be both vulnerable and supportive. Names and plans for the future reveal much about who and whose we are, where we have been, and where we might want to be going. What we plan for the future guides what we are doing today. Carefully designed interactive instruction can empower learners to be prepared for almost any career path they choose because communicating clearly is a benefit in any setting. See the website, https://planningwithpurpose.info/, for more specific ways to adapt your teaching in a virtual community of learners.

Chapter Four

Crossing into Novel Territory—
Reading Contemporary Fiction

In Robert Newton Peck's award-winning novel, a young boy queries his father:

> "Fences are funny, aren't they, Papa?"
> "How so?"
> "Well, you be friends with Mr. Tanner. Neighbors and all. But we keep this fence up like it was war. I guess that humans are the only things on earth that take everything they own and fence it off."
> "I never looked at it that way."
> "Time you did."[1]

In this twentieth-century novel, father and son discuss how human beings create "fences," including physical and social walls between ethnic groups, generations, and individuals. Your older teens and adult students have noticed such fences and are striving to learn about those who live across the fences in their own lives but may be reluctant to cross those metaphorical boundaries. They see in the media issues related to gender, race, ethnicity, language, social class, disability, age, and religion. Because books, as Rudine Sims Bishop describes them, can be windows, mirrors, or sliding glass doors, reading contemporary fiction can provide ways to look through, over, and around the fences that may both divide and protect.

Peck's moving novel offers a peek into the world of a twelve-year-old boy who wonders about the real value of socially constructed fences, some of which he wants to tear down, others of which he comes to understand, if not accept. This chapter offers ideas for teaching contemporary novels in ways that you can adapt to a full-length work of fiction in the course you teach.

DuValle Daniel, who teaches in a community college near Seattle, invites her students to read, discuss, reflect on, and write about books relating to issues of diversity and social justice. You'll see a list of recommended texts in chapters 5 and 8. She probably finds that the diverse students she teaches connect with many of the stories but resist others defensively.

For some students, peeking across the fence into a world can be like a trip to another planet where you can view, venture into, and explore new territories. In Peck's book, the narrator's father, Vermont farmer Haven Peck, makes ends meet in the late 1920s by slaughtering pigs for others to eat. The young boy considers several questions about his father. Why does the elder Peck earn a living that way? Do people really have to kill and eat pigs? Peck's son has to come to terms with adult reality.

Novels written in the twenty-first century help readers discover other contemporary people and cultures. While it can be frightening and confusing for some adults to traverse them, reading about life beyond one's fences can also be insightful, engaging, and relevant to their understanding of others. Sometimes the apparent distance between reality and fantasy makes the latter a safe way to discuss tough issues in diverse classroom settings. So, feel free to include fantasy and science fiction in your reading lists.

As an educator, you have the honor of and responsibility for guiding students across fences into stories about other people and places and helping your learners to engage various literary forms and challenging themes. Your thoughtful selection of texts can inspire students to interpret, understand, and respond critically to literary works by persons of different races, religions, and cultures in the context of students' own multimedia lives as they cross literary fences into novel territory.

This chapter explains how you can teach modern literature utilizing strategies described by the California Reading and Literacy Project. On their website, you will find methods, materials, and management ideas for doing so.

MOVING INTO, THROUGH, AND BEYOND A BOOK

Get into the book by:

- Encouraging students to make initial predictions
- Providing background information
- Identifying text-related vocabulary

Work through the book by:

- Reading aloud to the students
- Having students read aloud and silently during class
- Challenging students through active reading
- Guiding students to write about the work

- Connecting the book to students' lives
- Fostering class discussion with student- and teacher-generated questions

Move beyond the book by:

- Assessing student comprehension with performance or product options (or both)
- Assigning projects and essays
- Getting students involved in research about the book and its culture(s)
- Inspiring students to read more[2]

As you read further in this chapter, you can add to your suitcase of knowledge, preparing yourself to teach ways that contemporary authors employ the essential elements of fiction. Here are concrete examples from Peck's novel to demonstrate how you can reach and revive readers with skills and literacies to flourish in today's multicultural, multimedia societies.

PREPLANNING THE UNIT

To ease your anxiety, if you are teaching a book for the first time, estimate how much class time you need to spend on the book. Consider the following:

- Your department's homework guidelines and curricular goals
- The reading, writing, and thinking standards of your course
- The interests, skills, and needs of your students, as revealed in their work on earlier assignments
- How many pages of fiction reading your particular students can handle each week (consider how long it took YOU to read it and recognize that you may be a much stronger reader than your students)

Then plan a reading schedule before launching the unit. Few things clog up a unit more than unprepared students. You know yours; plan for them.

Building Background

Depending on the book you are teaching, you may find it useful to bring in picture e-books to supplement your lessons. If e-books aren't available, go "old school" and check hard copies out from your local library. For example, to prepare for or to expand the conversation about fences and society, bring in and share *Talking Walls*, written by Margy Burns Knight and illustrated by Anne Sibley O'Brien.[3] Use it to launch discussions about figurative walls and fences used to separate or protect or both. Robert Frost's poem "Mending Wall" would be another good lead in and is readily available online.[4] Other graphics you find online can provide background information about people, places, and events that help students better understand the fictional works you may choose to explore.

Deciding What Vocabulary

Vocabulary study is a topic to consider pedagogically before and during students' reading. For example, if you did not grow up on a farm, you may lack experience of the smells and sounds mentioned in Peck's novel set in rural Vermont. The same may be true for your students and the text you are teaching. What sensory experiences can you provide to enhance the understanding of your text? Remember, what you do in the classroom either helps or hinders your students' comprehension of the texts they encounter and explore outside of class doing homework or research for future lessons. Nothing is too basic if it deepens thinking.

Whichever twenty-first century book you use for class, be sure to introduce the students to the cultural language of the text; identify vocabulary students might not know, and determine how best to provide definitions or elicit definitions from them. Note particular words that may be unique to the book. Showing pictures illustrating vocabulary is particularly helpful for those raised in different cultures or just unfamiliar with the setting of your text.

Vocabulary your learners need to add to their speaking and writing vocabulary can be handled differently. Consider what words students need to know in order to read the opening chapters of this book; other books set for this course; and general reading in this course and others they may take. Encourage students to check print or digital dictionaries and then write their own one-sentence definitions that fit the context of their reading. Understanding context is an important concept to teach. It is not necessary to have students learn all the definitions of every vocabulary word on the list. Focus instead on the word meanings that help them understand this particular piece of literature.

Journaling by Video: Record It!

If students are already interested and motivated, you might want to allow groups of two or three students to make video recordings based on their written journals. You can ask them to meet online or at a site on campus and record a scene from the book as though they were creating an audio book with a dramatic scene. Using most digital cameras, they can save and upload it to your class online platform, and you can view and show it in class. The ideal length for these video dramatic readings is about two or three minutes.

For assessment, remind your budding video producers that video journals should display neatness—clear images, good visual grammar—and should be edited for pacing to enable the viewer-listener to follow along. Video journals should also exhibit clear diction, correct pronunciation, and correct spelling in written information.

Covering Is Not the Same as Teaching

Until students can understand and engage a text, you are not ready to go on to the next piece of literature. Even with a modern text, moving too quickly leads to superficial student understandings. On the other hand, moving too slowly misses opportunities for greater textual engagement. We believe that there are many ways to draw students into literature, but sometimes what you think will be the perfect selection for your class to read may end up being one that students just don't relate to. Sticking with a text that has clearly lost students' interest can also be counterproductive. So, determine students' critical abilities, monitor their progress, and make appropriate scheduling and pedagogical adjustments as you go.

You can help students read more deeply, critically, and efficiently as you teach them (or remind them of) a range of strategies to increase their reading comprehension. Depending on their past school experience, your students may already be familiar with some of these ideas. But, because current students seem to have a more positive attitude about more recently written literature, it often is better to teach and build on these approaches to reading literature while working with a contemporary book rather than with an established classic novel or complex poetry. Reviewing what has been taught is an efficient use of time, especially if you present the same information in new ways.

GETTING INTO THE BOOK

A great place to begin a unit on the novel is by having students create a "novels" section in their written journals, or a new folder on the digital one, and then create subsections for the various texts that you assign throughout the course. Their reading journal is a personal place for them to write their own reading summaries, responses, reflections, vocabulary study, diagrams and drawings along with questions like those mentioned in chapter 2.

Framing the Lesson to Launch the Reading

Consider, too, the ideas shared by Alison (Fastov) Taylor, a veteran educator who began her professional teaching at a hospital for emotionally and psychologically challenged students. Her introduction to teaching came during two years of working with twenty-five high-school students in a residential treatment program at Timberlawn Psychiatric Hospital in Dallas, Texas. Following a move to Washington, DC, she went on to teach at a highly competitive college prep school. Over time she refined a strategy called "FRAMES," which is explained below.

Alison believes vivid connection with students creates stronger engagement. The more thought and interest teachers invest in framing the text, assignment, or challenge, the better the students' understanding and outcome.

After learning the acronym FRAME, we recommend you share this with your students.

- F stands for "*Focus* on the topic" of the text
- R stands for "*Reveal* main ideas" in the text
- A stands for "*Analyze* details" set forth by the author (consider what aspect, idea, unique experience, or surprising piece of information is contained in the paragraph, article, chapter, or lesson)
- M stands for "making *Meaning* for ME," the reader (why is it important for me to know this or what has this to do with me, the reader?)
- E stands for "*Extending* understanding" (in what ways does this text connect to something I know from experience, observation, reading, hearing, or viewing in another course, in the news, or on social media)[5]

Taylor further recommends prepping that includes developing an introductory question, quotation, photo, cartoon, or social-media post that promises to arouse curiosity. Often some high-visibility or local-issue headline, YouTube video, or sports or celebrity event will generate lively opinions that can be directed, guided, or connected toward the subject or main idea of the piece.

Finally, ask students to write a one- or two-sentence "takeaway"—some key idea, conclusion, or possible direction this initial section suggests. Sharing them allows students to confirm or expand their own insights. As the teacher, avoid making specific comments on these. Leave their thoughts open, so, as students read on and read more, they form their own analyses and conclusions.

Playing Online Audio and Video Files

If quality readings of a selected book's opening are available online, select and play excerpts from them in class. YouTube and other video-posting websites sometimes include author readings or acceptable fan readings. Public libraries offer, on loan, audiobooks free with library cards. Avoid performance video clips that might frame the book visually for students before they have developed their own mental pictures of characters and settings. Chances are you have one or two tech-savvy students who can find recordings, download them, and bring them to you for previewing before playing them for their peers. Remember, what is done in your class reflects you.

Begin lessons on journaling with a random romp through the selected book, as described in chapter 2, or with open questions to familiarize your students with this particular text. Questions might include the following:

1. Do you recall a book that grabbed you from the first sentence?
2. How would you define a "novel" in ways other than length that make it different from a short story?

Consider posing broad perspectives relating to your particular text from the myriad online sources that suggest questions such as:

1. What is the relationship between decisions and consequences?
2. What allows some individuals to take a stand against prejudice or oppression while others choose to participate in it?
3. How are people transformed through their relationships with others?

Try to create an open, exciting experience for students while monitoring responses to questions that make your readers feel ill at ease. Resist commenting on their responses, even with facial expressions. Encourage honesty; insist on courtesy. Demonstrate what you teach.

Your opening attitude sets the tone for the class. If students know that you enjoy fiction, they are more likely to read it expectantly. However, there is no reason to try to gin up false enthusiasm for a literary work you do not like. Even if you do not prefer reading fiction, you can share your enthusiasm for learning about something new. Of course, you want to allot time for them to read books they choose themselves.

Don't forget the amazing resource of audiobooks. As mentioned before, so many are available for free through the university or local public libraries. Nontraditional students, those who may not live on campus and have long commutes, often find they make good use of their time on the road by listening. So, continue to reward independent reading but avoid penalizing students who cannot do much independent reading. You know your college setting. Develop goals and help students develop skills and opportunities to reach them.

Few students take pleasure in a book if they do not understand the cultural context, time period, unusual references, and difficult vocabulary. So, before you assign them to read too far in the book, spark their critical interest in the story and give them some helpful tools to begin enjoying and discussing the text right away.

Sparking Critical Interest in the Story

You can ignite interest in the book and elicit visual interpretation by having students do something as simple as examining the cover art of a paperback

Inspire desire to explore new texts.
https://www.istockphoto.com/photo/two-boys-on-the-fence-looking-for-smth-gm104867934-7668637

or the drawing included with the text in your class anthology. Give the students two or three minutes to examine that art and print, individually or in small groups.

No cover illustration? Check online bookstores or the publisher's website to see if you can find cover images for past paperback or hardcover editions. Even without a cover image, it's worth discussing the book design graphics. In this case, you could ask students the following:

1. Why do you think the publishers chose certain fonts, font sizes, colors, or word placements?
2. What is the name of the font(s)?
3. Why may there be no graphics—photos, drawings, or other artwork?
4. What does the book blurb on the cover or reviewer comments make you think about this book?
5. Where else do you hear or read comments about the arts (e.g., movie trailers and newspaper or web ads for movies)?

These metatextual strategies—ways of talking about how texts communicate—create curiosity about the book. They also encourage the groups of students to own their learning, since they clearly can learn from one another as well as from you. Students soon discover that it is educationally good to formulate and express opinions, reasonable interpretations, and evaluations of texts. This is what good readers do.

Finally, students who think only classic writing should be analyzed soon learn that modern texts can be examined as well as enjoyed—and that criticism can lead to greater enjoyment. In this case, criticism should not be limited to simple statements of opinions. Encourage students to expand their opinion statements with specific reasons. Remember, students do not have to like a literary work in order to appreciate it. See explanations of the "Nine Yardsticks of Value" in chapter 2 and in the chart in chapter 6.

Locate and display images of the time period or part of the country, or both, to create intrigue. Consider bringing in items to suggest characters or events ahead of time and just setting them up on a table or desk that students have to pass when they enter the room. Sometimes a short poem on one of the topics in the books is just the thing to jump-start a book. Occasionally, projecting a photograph or piece of artwork will suffice.

Using Student-Produced Slides to Facilitate Discussion

As you begin the discussion with students, write on the board one- or two-word summaries of their initial thoughts and feelings about the book. If students generally arrive with their laptops or tablets, pause for a few moments for students to create a simple PowerPoint slide that contains one of these short summaries using font and background colors designed to match the meaning of the summary. Inviting students to consider graphics in light of their reading encourages them to note ways the author uses words to recreate sensory experiences.

This ten-minute activity gives students time to practice skills they are learning for future multimodal presentations. Because students learn in different ways, based on innate intelligence, as seen in the research of Howard Gardner, seeing how others depict what is read supports your visual learners and optimizes the skills of students who show best what they know through sketching and diagramming what they see when they read.

Fonts and colors can "speak" to readers even though these visual images are not as precise as "word language." This kind of assignment teaches media grammar, too. Check out "Reading the Media" in chapter 6 or online sites to help familiarize yourself with media grammar if this is a new concept for you. Students interested in drama might want to speak the word(s) interpretively as a looping soundtrack for each image their group creates.

Your tech-savvy students may be interested in experimenting with a version of the Pecha Kucha format as a final project. Simply put, Pecha Kucha involves creating twenty slides, which are set to advance every twenty seconds as a speaker narrates. You may decide to create and model this format to introduce the contemporary novel to supplement your instruction for a piece of literature and then make this format an optional student assignment later in the school year. Note this concept of choice in the recommendations of Stefani Boutelier, which are described later in this chapter,

Finally, students doing multislide presentations (one word or phrase per slide) can add a soundtrack that relates to the novel's subject or characters. Students may wish to create one for the novel you are studying together. PowerPoint's player function creates a short "motion picture" that sets a pre-reading benchmark for later review. If students enjoy seeing the PowerPoint presentation in class, consider showing it again at the end of the unit to discuss initial versus later impressions of the novel. Reshowing these slides makes for valuable pre-exam review, too.

Caution: Do take time to create these kinds of slides yourself to see what skills and time are needed to complete them. You may find the depth of thinking and reflecting required are worth the time you allot for such alternative ways to look at and depict various genres of literature.

Applying Something Old to Something New

How about adapting one of those "KWL" charts that students probably used in high school? This graphic organizer that asks students what they *know*, *want* to learn, and have *learned* can be useful in classes with adult college students, too. Working with the familiar makes the unfamiliar less daunting. It's like seeing a McDonald's sign in the middle of the desert.

What do students know about Vermont (or the setting of your book); about the Shakers (or a social, regional, or racial group in your book); about the origins of baseball (or a cultural event in your book); about this historical period; and so on? What do they hope to discover as they read? Save completing the K column for later in the unit. An opening class activity during the time that you are reading the book could be to spend a few minutes filling in the L column or adding to the W column. If the book does not reveal answers to these questions, these questions could be the basis of a final project or performance in which students conduct brief research and then share in a written or artistic way what they learn. What this really indicates is the importance of selecting a full-length book to read together that is a rich trove in which students can find examples of the literary and rhetorical devices you are required to teach.

Organizing Quotations as an Opening Activity

1. Photocopy a randomized list of quotations from the book you plan to teach. (Leave off the page numbers.)
2. Ask the students to put the quotations in an order that makes sense to them.
3. Meet in pairs to compare the order. (Order is unimportant at this point. Thinking is.)
4. Then, talk briefly about what students think the book is about. What inferences can they make based simply on these quotations? (This is a good way to highlight the sentence structure and vocabulary the author uses, too.)

CROWD SOURCING: GATHER AND USE WHAT STUDENTS KNOW

Esther Gabay, who teaches in a college in New York City admits that students often do not know how much they know already. She says:

My students enter our community college first-year composition course with varied academic experiences and knowledge. Their ages range from eighteen to anywhere in adulthood, and they represent diverse demographics in terms of race, culture, nationality, religion, dis/ability, and language.

Through the years, I've learned that students have many different approaches to and feelings about reading. While many students know that active reading and note-taking are useful reading practices, they often have trouble exercising these practices while they read for class. So, in order to build on what students already know, and create a classroom culture that values slowing down and engaging in a deliberate reading process, I begin the course by crowdsourcing different active and critical reading strategies from students.

This teacher of adults in the community-college course recommends that class time be spent inviting students to describe ways that they use to read and make sense of a common text. First, she asks students to write a list of strategies they know or use and, then, when called upon, to read their list aloud. She writes the strategies on the board and usually garners dozens of approaches to making sense of texts. Once these approaches are gathered, students discuss them, then vote for strategies they will add to their lists because they believe the strategies will be useful to them.

Gabay assigns the students a new text to read for homework and encourages them to try out some of the strategies they learned about from their peers. At the next class meeting, students report on their experience and the class decides on the top five most useful ways to improve comprehension as they read texts. For the remainder of the course, they are encouraged to strengthen their reading using strategies they learned from their classmates. Her student learners are empowered by their crowdsourcing, speaking, sharing, and experimenting with various strategies and then settling on approaches to unlocking texts that work best for them.

ALLOWING AUTHORS TO SPEAK FOR THEMSELVES

While it is important to provide some background for the book, initially it is good to let the text speak for itself. Allow your students to engage with the text and create their own meaning. Provide students only the information that they need to understand the beginning of the story. Then, as the story unfolds, supply additional information. Even if you have had to do a lot of research yourself to prepare to teach an unfamiliar book, remember not to inundate the students with all of your new-found knowledge—TMI.

Too much information can overshadow or even bury the book. It can definitely kill the pleasure of reading it. On a trip, it would be like touring five different museums on the same day! Such an overload of information would be just too much to permit appreciation of the craftsmanship of those whose work is on display. The focus should be on the reader as well as the text. Meaning comes from student interaction with the text.

A host of textbooks, websites, academic books, and colleagues can help inform your own understanding of the text; however, during class, resist dumping all this new-found knowledge on the students. Rather, first focus on the basic aspects of the time and place that students need to know to figure out the plot, setting, and characters in the novel. In carefully selected, engaging books of fiction and nonfiction, the authors can speak for themselves.

WORKING THROUGH THE BOOK

Plan alternative ways to work through the texts based on what you know about your students: their time, access to technology, prior knowledge, and learning styles. Consider the five senses and active lessons as you differentiate your classroom instruction and assessments.

Listening to Reading Aloud

Think about how often you and your peers purchase or borrow audio books or attend events where authors read from their books. So, it is not surprising that an appealing way to begin teaching a text is to read portions aloud to your students. This gives unengaged readers a chance to learn by listening and following along. It supports English-language learners because it helps them confirm the sound of the language with the printed words. Reading aloud also models pacing, pronunciation, and inflection . . . and allows the listener to bring the story alive and visualize the scene.

Did you know that some readers do not visualize scenes or characters as they read to themselves? Their focus is entirely on decoding and absorbing information without allowing themselves to be or knowing how to be transported by a book. Reading aloud to them and pausing occasionally for them to acknowledge what they're seeing, hearing, and thinking helps them develop this important reading skill—imagination.

Since some international students' first language uses a non-English style alphabet, they might need practice associating sounds with the written English letters as they work to improve their reading literacy. Hearing the words as they follow the text is another way to increase this association and expand their comprehension. Nancy (Perkins) Kohl, who taught international students at the University of Massachusetts, shares the suggestions described in the following paragraph for active listening.

Try connecting early on with students' multiple intelligences by assigning different activities for them to do while listening in class. Some might sketch in their journals what is happening in the story or jot notes in a chart with story events. Many multitasking students prefer to listen to music while studying. Since there is no "right" way to read, as long as students are keeping up and comprehending the text, engage non-aural learners with appropriate ways to formulate and express textual interpretations. Consider playing instrumental music during silent reading time. Music played in a rhythm that matches the beat of the heart at rest calms listeners and helps them to focus.

Reading Silently Has Value

While reading aloud to students is good pedagogy, students also need to be able to learn by reading silently. You can help students stay on schedule by providing in-class reading periods. Doing so eliminates the frustration for students who are unable to participate in class discussions simply because they are behind on reading. Consider having a prompt or question written or projected on the board before students arrive. Then ask them to use the first five-to-seven minutes of class to peruse their reading to find text evidence to support their answer or just to catch up on the reading.

As students write, circulate among them while taking attendance but also stop near individuals, adding to your own notes indications of student engagement in the task. Journaling in this simple writing activity focuses students on the day's topic while you complete record-keeping.

Observing students' responses and watching them read also can help you identify students who may be experiencing difficulties. Pay attention to how long it takes individuals to complete a page of reading. Remember, your

Listening: another way to experience the writer's words.
https://www.istockphoto.com/photo/attractive-young-man-reading-book-while-listening-to-music-on-white
  -head-phones-gm839374776-136681319

students might not read as quickly as you. You might consider using an initial timed reading activity to help you monitor the pace of your lesson. Be sure to assure them that this is simply to help you with planning. In no way will it be used to grade or rank them. Again, the importance of sharing WHY.

Now, have your students read for five minutes and then note how many pages they got through. Have them record how many pages they read on small notecards or slips you provided with their names and quietly collect the notecards or slips without discussion. You might be amazed to find that some complete two to three pages while others complete ten or more. It is for this reason that it is wiser to give the last ten to twenty minutes of the class for reading.

Too often when educators think ten minutes is plenty of time for everyone to read a short piece, it isn't enough. Many may finish, but there are always those who need fifteen or twenty minutes more—or longer. Meanwhile, these false assumptions mean the class cannot proceed with the lesson and students must wait. If you have concerns, but not the expertise to address them yourself, seek the assistance of a reading specialist or the advice of the department chair or a colleague.

Reading Dramatically in Pairs or Groups

Occasionally, give students the chance to read aloud with the whole class, in small groups, or to a partner. Reading aloud is an important skill and part of public speaking, but it is different from reading silently—and even done in different parts of the brain. That is why a person can sometimes fluently read aloud an entire story without comprehending what was read.

Students who especially dislike reading aloud may need to practice in a nonthreatening setting. You can invite such students to read aloud short passages of their choosing just to you; you can track their progress and encourage them personally. Remind students that public speaking skills are important for most careers, and reading aloud can help them practice their articulation (clear pronunciation of words). Students work harder at it if they know that reading aloud is a significant step toward career success. For English-language learners with access to recent technology, encourage them to read aloud on a talk-to-text program to confirm their pronunciation improvements.

Of course, you have the hams, too, who just love to play parts from the book. The dialogue in the text provides exceptional ways for students to gain insight into the personalities of the characters in the story. Encourage dramatic oral reading or consider using "readers theater," which asks students to select scenes made up of mostly dialogue and script them out as a play. All description between speaking parts becomes the role of the narrator and is scripted as such. Every word is included. No words are added, and none are omitted. Once the text is scripted, students then read their parts without any dramatic action or flourishes. All meaning comes from inflection.

Whatever method you use, be fair and have students take turns reading aloud the most popular characters. You may wish to serve as the narrator if you want to ensure that the reading stays on track.

READING ACTIVELY

It is essential for students' expanded education that they become critical readers. Students know that people read books for fun, but they might not realize how often adults also read fiction and nonfiction simply to enrich their lives. In short, students who read widely and attentively deepen their understanding of different cultures as well as the human condition. Students benefit when they learn that active reading requires careful attention to the text, regardless of the medium—print or electronic, aural or visual. In travel, it's like learning to read the road signs, those with words and those with universal symbols. It helps you get where you're going without getting lost . . . too many times.

One essential skill in active reading is recognizing how subparts of a larger text relate to one another. These text structures, sometimes called "rhetorical structures," include descriptive, sequential, enumerative, cause-effect, problem-solution, and compare-contrast relationships within a text. Readers of fiction sometimes are surprised by how often fiction writers incorporate many of these same devices.

Assuming Personae in Fiction and in Biographical Writing

Once they have "met" the main characters, ask your students to sign up to keep a journal from their chosen or assigned character's perspective and write two- or three-sentence entries for each section of assigned reading. Provide in-class time for small-group meetings of those writing from the same character's point of view. Mix it up some days and construct groups with different characters meeting together to talk for a few moments about the way their character is addressing the problems in the book.

1. Is he or she making wise or foolish choices?
2. Is he or she assisting or thwarting the protagonist?
3. Is he or she like or different from someone the student knows?

If your learners have enjoyed this personae perspective, you could follow up their reading of the book with an assignment that asks them to connect their character with current events and answer questions like "What would your chosen character have to say about something in the news today?"; "What issues would interest them?"; or "What television shows or movies would that person like?"

When students read fiction, they enter into a story created by the author. They let the author transport them into a projected, imaginary "world." To accomplish this world-projecting storytelling, authors create the following:

- relationships among characters
- characters' motivation
- causal relationships between characters' thoughts and actions

Because of these author-created structures—along with readers' own real-life relationships—students begin to predict certain things will occur in the story. As they learn more about the structure of these longer works, students' expectations rise in similar ways.

Tracking Character Development

Students wonder why characters think and act in certain ways. As they read, they speculate about why particular events lead to other events—like the age-old conundrums about why bad things happen to good people. Adult learners often begin mentally asking the same kinds of questions about fiction as they ask about life, and college teachers can help the learners develop strategies to help comprehend, interpret, and evaluate their reading. As they gain skills to identify and examine the impact of intra-text structures in their own reading, students engage in the story or article as if conversing with the author and the characters.

Continue to encourage students to record in their journals any questions that arise when reading.

Prompting for Journal Writing

So, how do students move from the book itself toward a more critical dialogue with it? The conversation has to start somewhere, but some of your students will not have practiced taking notes when they see a movie, play a YouTube video, listen to an audio book, or read fiction. Therefore, keeping a reader-response journal can effectively initiate a student's personal dialogue with a text.

In this type of journal, students do the following:

- Transcribe or copy important passages
- Record their own questions about the text
- Note what they enjoy in the text
- Indicate important material for later study
- Record what they're thinking, feeling, or reminded of during the reading

Students also can journal in their textbooks with sticky notes so they do not have to recopy the text sections in their journals. Some e-books have features for inserting annotations, too. Then students can copy those thoughts into their separate journal notebook, save or copy into their digital journals, while keeping the sticky notes or electronic notations for quick reference in their books.

You might even suggest that students use different color techniques to code story elements or text structure and log their reactions, especially their questions. Propose that students use a specific color to note passages that strike them as potentially effective video or audio scenes for later recording. Here, also, is a place to use emojis to record graphic responses to reading.

Invite students to visualize what is going on in the book based on the author's direct and indirect statements. Remember when we talked about the importance of imagining or seeing the scene? Drawing maps and pictures in their journals helps some students develop or hold on to those visualizations. Some students working online may find themselves doing searches to view items or places mentioned in their reading. Encourage such exploration; it enriches comprehension and expands the overall reading experience, especially when they share their drawings with peers.

HIGHLIGHTING ACADEMIC VOCABULARY

What about terms in the text that the students should be adding to their own speaking and writing vocabulary? What about words used in the book that also appear in reading and conversations your students have in other classes? And what about general academic vocabulary used primarily in college classes? You can help students learn the meanings of and connections among words by identifying such academic words on their vocabulary list and asking students themselves to find the definitions in print or online dictionaries. Directing them to do this on their own takes the onus off of you and makes them self-directed learners. Adult students in general education classes may be surprised to discover how much what they are learning with you is empowering them to read more critically in their other courses, on their jobs, and with their family members.

Invite students to alphabetically list the words with their definitions on a class website or post comparative definitions on a class online document. The shared document itself serves as a kind of study sheet students can print out or download to their own computers. The words that are specific to the text, though, are those for which you can provide definitions.

Like many veteran educators, you may find it productive to maintain a word chart to which you add new words throughout the course. Seeing is believing. As students enter the classroom, have the words projected onto the screen. Students notice the list and catch on to the fact that it is important to learn and use the words in their discussions and in writing about the text. This experience is like seeing the same advertisement on road signs while on a trip. Soon you remember them and may even decide to visit the site or purchase the product. The same can happen with your students. What they see, they remember; what they remember, they are likely to use.

Challenge your students to use their vocabulary regularly even if they are teased for their increased sophistication and even if they earn higher grades for doing so.

Dividing the Labor Can Multiply the Results

If the vocabulary in the book you are reading is particularly challenging for one reason or another, allot in-class time for vocabulary work. Since most students love to talk anyway, create small groups who will be responsible for just a few of the words on the list. For example, if your list contains twenty words, have five groups who each are responsible for showing the meaning of four words. In addition to the traditional information usually required in vocabulary study, add photos that can be uploaded into a computer program and then projected in a digital presentation. This kind of alternative activity reinforces learning and is a valuable use of fifteen minutes of class time.

Calling on Cell Phones for Vocabulary Study—A Mini-Assignment

Invite students to use their cell phones to complete this assignment. Doing so reminds them of a resource for learning that most of them have with them all the time.

1. Locate the assigned word in the text being studied.
2. Determine how it is used (what part of speech) in the context of the literary work.

3. Use a cell phone to locate the word in a dictionary that includes more than synonyms.

4. Search on a phone app or use a cell-phone camera to photograph images to help classmates understand the meaning of each assigned word. The image should reflect the literal and/or figurative meaning and will serve as a mnemonic for the word. Alternatively, consider color, font, image, or music to portray the meaning of the word, as used in the context of the literary work being studied.

5. Then, as a group, create a one-to-two-minute slide or video presentation that reflects what the group has learned about the words, including original sentences using the words and one or more of the synonyms, antonyms, and appositives to help clarify the meaning.

This assignment utilizes the range of skills of a typical group of students who have varying types of intelligence; it has active and passive tasks that appeal to students with different personalities and with varying levels of English-language proficiency.

The assignment is sure to be a success if you do the following:

- Design the lessons carefully
- Have written instructions to supplement the oral ones
- Demonstrate a sample product with the class helping you gather information on one vocabulary word
- Allow ten to fifteen minutes of class time during the final fifteen minutes of class during the first week that literature is being studied
- Set a digital timer each day to reserve the closing fifteen minutes for small-group work and five minutes for clearing up and closing the lesson for the day

During these two or three weeks reading this novel together, begin your class lessons as usual, orienting students to the literary work; provide historical background and personal information about the author, and remind students of the language of literature they already know. Then, use the remainder of class for a few days for this kind of vocabulary work. After starting a task in class, if appropriate for your school setting, assign completing the task as collaborative homework.

It's worth the in-class time for such group work and language study. It can be an opportunity to do no-stress formative assessments of your students that will help you adjust your instruction as you plan for further lessons. It gives students time to do what they do best: work together and learn from one another while exploring and applying skills that lead to meeting a range of general-education course standards.

DEVELOPING DIVERSE PERSONAL
CONNECTIONS TO CONTEMPORARY NOVELS

The key to teaching novels is helping students to recognize three things.

1. A novelist's imaginative story is usually a mirror for some people even if it is not a mirror for others, such as your students.
2. Students can discover that other people's mirrors can serve as windows for getting to know those who are different from themselves. Windows become venues for self-understanding as students begin to see similarities among those they read about and those with whom they live.
3. Reading about others enables students to see what human beings have in common, across their cultural fences.

Novels express not only cultural particularities of time and place but also common aspects of the human condition, such as fear and loneliness, joy and delight, agreement and disagreement. For instance, adolescents in every culture eventually come of age; the process is universal even though it takes different cultural forms. Metaphorical windows can help students simultaneously to understand themselves, their communities, other persons, and other communities.

Relating through Personal Connections

As mentioned earlier, textual literacy includes the ability to relate fictional worlds to one's own life. These reader-to-self, reader-to-world, or reader-to-text relationships can work in multiple ways. Yes, they can serve as mirrors and windows, but sometimes also as sliding glass doors that do both, reflecting and providing a way in or out. Include options to read nonfiction, like biographies and autobiographies, and see your skeptical readers bloom into eager ones.

Encourage conversation but guide it so it does not become denigrating or disrespectful of what is different or simply unfamiliar. Choosing culturally relevant books and articles means more than selecting writing by and about the ethnicities represented in your community, college, or classroom. It also means choosing literature that introduces your students to those groups not represented where you reside and thus expands your students' experience.

Shanika Carter is an adjunct professor who teaches at Grand Valley State University in West Michigan. In a single school year, she may have community-college-level students, including high-school students who are dual-enrolled in college courses, as well as four-year-university-level students. Carter's classes are diverse and include those who commute from urban Muskegon and rural areas around the colleges in Central Michigan.

Carter notes, "I have become more proactive with incorporating real-life, current news and media issues in my curriculum, along with referencing some of the texts I have used in the past for the history and theory components. This is especially the case with topics related to culture, diversity, generational groups, and gender orientation, particularly when teaching in the more rural areas of Michigan."

Her choices of texts, she says, seem to increase student interest in their writing. The students are more eager to become student group leaders, sharing their experiences as reflected or influenced by the texts they are reading together. Carter says she sees a "spark" in their eyes as they incorporate into their own creations what they are reading and learning about published writing. Their enthusiasm for reading and writing is making her love what she's doing.

Earl H. Brooks, an assistant professor of English in Baltimore, Maryland, shared with us that one of the teaching challenges he encountered was increasing the depth and rigor of class discussions in an introductory college course in rhetoric and composition.

To show the relevancy of texts to an issue like social justice, Brooks told us that he links each reading to some form of media, such as documentaries, films, television series, or music. For example, by devoting a small portion of class time to a documentary, such as *LA 92* (2017), "I can pull students into that historical moment and thus heighten the sense of relevance for readings from writers who responded to the Los Angeles riots of 1992. I aim to build excitement and drama for each reading assignment in ways that will not only encourage students to read through sheer curiosity, but also emphasize the relationship between any particular reading and the social dramas of our current moment." We encourage you to do the same.

Honoring Student Privacy

Ask students to journal about their personal connections with the world of the book; such journaling promotes discussion because students articulate in writing thoughts they can then paraphrase out loud. Just remember that some students are reticent about reading or discussing their reflections with the entire class. Respect their privacy, and you can gain their trust and motivate them to read deeply and write honestly.

Remind them that, if what you read in their responses makes you believe they are a danger to themselves or others, you are bound by law to report it to authorities. In addition, caution students about posting personal information online since privacy is a major issue in the information age. One of the reasons that social networking websites, such as Facebook, are so popular is that students think they regulate who they allow to access their postings by approving who their "friends" are—those who can access their website. But no public site is totally secure, and what is posted today as a lark may be embarrassing or even dangerous tomorrow.

Privacy and tact are important literary issues; openness and honesty are essential to building trust in the classroom. So, write in your own journal frequently, right along with your students. Doing so not only models this kind of writing but also reminds you of what it is like to reveal text-to-self connections with others. Then sometimes share with them what you've written.

Share with your students some of the experiences you have had with your parents, siblings, and friends—and also admit that there are some experiences you would, and they should, not write about online. If you respect students' privacy, they are more likely to share their journals with you—and they learn that responding to readings should be an ethical as well as an academic practice. In other words, invite rather than insist that they share or show to others what they write.

INSPIRING CLASS DISCUSSION

Educators often approach the study of a book or article by giving students a list of discussion questions found in their anthologies. These questions can effectively ease students into the reading and demonstrate the types of questions and ideas that they should be considering. However, "check your comprehension" or "for further discussion" questions are text based and often avoid asking readers to engage with the readings. You will foster better and more engaging discussions by encouraging students to write their own thoughtful, life-connected, and text-connected questions. Plus, they're kind of impressed to think their questions are better than those in the book.

Regardless of how you settle on the questions, try a variety of discussion group formats: pairs, small groups, and whole class. Some students are more inclined to read their journal entries and discuss personal responses to the text if they are in smaller groups. Still, many like to push the envelope, test the boundaries, and interject topics that are on the edge—just for fun or attention—so it is important to circulate among them as they read and talk about their writing.

If a student offers an inappropriate remark, then a moment's eye contact, a subtle head shake, or a quiet admonition from you should be enough to refocus the discussion. As on a road trip, when the sheriff is spotted, drivers adjust their driving behavior—and so do your students; when you are nearby, they are reminded of the rules of the road as they pertain to the class.

Interspersing Literature Circles

Think about setting up literature circles, a discussion strategy often attributed to Harvey "Smokey" Daniels, as a way to explore a few chapters in the book your class is studying together. For this approach to reading and discussing literature, you create small groups of five or six students and assign or let them draw role names or numbers to perform certain tasks. The following are among the many ways to structure literature circle responsibilities:

- Making connections between what students haves read already and the book they currently are reading
- Pointing out ways words on the vocabulary list are being used
- Selecting a particularly interesting, humorous, or thought-provoking passage to read aloud to the members of the group
- Drawing a picture of a scene that is crucial to the plot or understanding of a character
- Bringing in an appropriate prop that illustrates an incident or symbolizes a character
- Keeping time to assure that the group completes the tasks in the allotted time

The tasks can vary depending on the book you have chosen. See online sources for ways to schedule literature circles about various texts.

Adapting Think, Pair, Share Strategies

Have students work independently to reflect on and think about a prompt, then pair students up to talk with a partner before one or both of them shares with or reports to the whole class. This is an effective way to begin discussions about difficult passages or controversial topics, especially with shy students or those who tend to leap over into the driver's seat if not kept in their seat belts. Consider adding another layer to this familiar strategy by recommending that students find support for their responses in the text you may be having them read that day.

As the students are writing their answers, you could circulate among them, looking over their shoulders, seeing who goes directly to a likely place in the text to find the answer. Don't be surprised if they go to an unexpected section and still come up with a valid response. When you notice that the majority of the students have something written, you could call on the ones who have different, but valid, maybe even opposing answers. Then ask the class who agrees that student A's answer seems logical and who thinks that student B's answer seems stronger. You could follow up by asking students to find additional evidence from the text that supports the answer of student A or student B.

Of course, modeling first and providing answer stems can help students get started. An example students may recognize from Gary D. Schmidt's *The Wednesday Wars* may inspire them to do this kind of writing:

"I believe Mrs. Baker is . . . because . . . and this section on page . . . supports my observation."

Or, "Character A is a jerk . . . because . . . and when you look at page . . . you'll see that I'm right."

Or, "The passage on page . . . suggests the principal is prejudiced . . . because of the way the author uses negative images."[6]

Even though you may decide to conduct whole-class discussions, you still could incorporate some of the literature-circle roles. If the majority of your students are reliable about completing homework, once you introduce the roles, invite students to sign up for the role they would like to play for the next literature-circle-type discussion. Then, assign for homework their gathering information to fill that role during the next class meeting.

During the next class, you could have the students playing the same roles meet to compare answers during the first ten minutes of class, then invite them as a panel to present their answers to the class. Or, after the small-group meeting, you could reconfigure the class so that each group includes at least one person fulfilling each role and have them "teach" that group what they learned.

You may know this organizational pattern as "jigsaw grouping." Each of these strategies increases student confidence about speaking out loud among their peers and deepens their understanding of the text. Your English-language learners may even flourish in these settings.

WRITING ABOUT A BOOK IN CLASS

Develop three questions about the recent reading, then ask students to answer one using specific references and selected quotations from a specified section. For example, have them refer to five of the seven chapters read so far and incorporate the illustrative facts and words smoothly into the text of their essay writing. Encourage answering the question in their thesis statement as part of their introductory paragraph, then writing two or three body paragraphs that make a hearty "PIE" (see explanation below) with lots of rich, meaty filling, concluding with a summary or reflection on what they have written in the body paragraphs.

In the PIE strategy, P stands for point: state your point or position in response to the prompt. I stands for illustration: support your point with two or three direct references to the story. One of these can be a short quotation: "For example . . .." (Give the page number in parenthesis following the reference or quotation.) E stands for explain: explain the connection between your illustrations and your point. "This shows . . .."

Periodically assign in-class writing for your students to practice thinking and writing skills that learners are required to demonstrate in most general-education courses across the content areas. This writing need not be graded. It's like the weightlifting that athletes do. It empowers them for something later. Let students show their skill level, so you'll know what they know now and what you need to teach next.

TESTING THOUGHTS ON THEME

Return now to examples from *A Day No Pigs Would Die*. One of the themes is that something may die in order for something else to live. When searching the novel, students find these examples: a cow nearly dies birthing the twin calves; a crow gobbles a frog; and the narrator's family eats animals they slaughter for food. Ultimately, Rob, the main character, suffers the death of his father and has to assist his mother with farm tasks, including killing his own pet pig so the family can have food to eat. A few students become so enamored of Rob's pet, Piggy, that they convert and become vegans—at least while studying the novel. Of course, even as vegans they consume formerly living things. All life depends on other life.

While studying a book, students can examine further concepts of theme—the overall message(s) of a text or what the text is trying to say about a topic. The concept of literature itself is sometimes defined by a work's universal themes about human nature and the human condition as well as by its aesthetic qualities. Themes, though, generally are considered to be statements about topics, not just the topics themselves; themes require a verb to indicate the author's viewpoint. "Life is grand" is a theme; "life" is a subject, but not a theme. "Fences make good neighbors" is a theme; "fences" is simply a topic. However, themes can also incorporate universal questions that all humans face, such as good versus evil, coming of age, or revenge. Note as well that novels often include multiple themes.

Your students may have been introduced to this kind of thinking about literature in their precollegiate classes. They may have used the "SWBST" approach. There they would fill in a graphic organizer in which they record what Somebody Wanted, But, So, and Then, to reflect the main characters, the conflict, the attempts to solve it, and then the resolution. Using this SWBST chart may be a good place to start and then move on to sentence statements about the book.

After you remind your students about the concept of universal themes, let them try to discern what may or may not be a universal theme expressed through the twenty-first-century novel you are studying together. Invite students to experiment with theme statements in their own reading and journaling. What is the story saying to them?

Also, ask them to test or verify their ideas about themes with specific, supporting examples from the beginning, middle, and the end of the novel. Students soon notice that most books have at least two or three overarching ideas that can be summarized in thematic statements that capture most individual responses to the text. In the biography or autobiography, what experiences are described that reflect what is true about people in general?

GRADING STUDENT RESPONSES TO A BOOK

Encourage formal and informal student responses to whatever genre or texts you teach. Since informal writing is more personal, students should earn full credit just for demonstrating that they have read the selected material and responded responsibly to the prompt. Formal writing, on the other hand, calls for more precise literary analysis and is graded for form and accuracy as well as content. Consider the following samples from student journals:

Student #1's journal essay was a "Five Ws and H Summary" (the journalistic who, what, where, why, when, and how) based on seven-to-ten verbs that describe the plot. This student wrote this entry after the class studied the elements of fiction and read a number of short stories for which students were writing this kind of summary.

Student Journal Entry #1

Robert cut school because he was made fun of. He found a cow who was in labor and birthing a calf. He is in Vermont, and 12 years old. He desperately tries to help the cow, because she is in pain and when the cow chokes, he reaches down her throat and pulls out the "goiter." She bites his arm and pulls him all around. His arm was gnawed, and flesh was missing. He gets stitches and after being in bed for about a week, he goes to help his pa. Their neighbor that owns the cow thanks Robert for helping her and gives him a pig! Robert is excited. His dad informs him of the care it takes to own a pig. Then they talk some more.

This student's response is complete because it includes all the elements in the prompt and what the student has written is true about the book. Grade options are a PLUS for complete and correct, a CHECK for complete but not all accurate, and a MINUS for failure to submit the work. This student earned a PLUS.

About a week after beginning a book, once students have closely read and discussed the exposition, your students should be ready to write personal responses, normally by answering "what" and "why" questions. Reading their personal responses helps you learn which parts of the story interest students as well as whether they are missing important details that would then need to be addressed in class.

Consider having students send their responses electronically the day before the next class meeting. Making such a due date, you can be more certain they'll be ready for class, and, equally, you'll have time to peruse their responses and adjust your lesson plans for the next class meeting. You also learn more about the students as people—which can help with planning subsequent lessons to better meet learners' academic needs and accommodate their varied interests.

To prepare students to write analytically, ask them to write journal entries in which they focus their attention on the elements of fiction or specific literary devices. Student #2 chose to write about symbols and similes and reveals understanding of the former but not the latter device.

Student Journal Entry #2
    Peck uses symbols as similes. On page number 104, it says, "And during fair week, I guess it's like a big brass band that can't stop playing." Another time he uses a symbol is still on page 104. It says, "Just like a mouth I know that's got blackberry all over it. These are both symbols in the book.

This incomplete journal entry does not include an explanation of why each of the quotations is a symbol or a simile. Fortunately, an educator who read this entry could see (before a test revealed) that this student needed help identifying the ways that authors use symbols and similes. After reviews in class, this student handled these kinds of questions well. However, the student earned only a CHECK for this assignment.

A third student rambled in his journal entry. But this entry revealed which incidents caught the student's attention and which ones needed clarification.

Student Journal Entry #3
    One of the things about this book is that it will start out with a conflict, then tell why that conflict arose. For instance, in the end of this section of the . . . (sic). There is a man that goes and digs up his daughter from her grave. I didn't really understand the whole conflict of why he couldn't dig her up. Oh, also we now have proof that Robert is a Shaker because he goes to the meetings. I'm amazed that a pig would get to be as big as twelve-year-old boys. Because unless they get any bigger than that I probably wouldn't believe it was unless I saw it.

Sometimes students ask questions in class; other times questions arise only in students' writing. This student earned a CHECK. All in all, student journals help teachers answer learners' questions and tailor future lessons as well.

ASSIGNING PROJECTS AND ESSAYS

When planning each assignment, determine what you need to know about student understanding and design product or performance assessments through which students can demonstrate that knowledge.

Differentiating Assessments

Recognize that students have various strengths, including different types of intelligence. Plan a wide variety of projects for assessing students so that their various types of intelligence can be used in at least some projects. Stefani Boutelier, a professor who teaches at a Catholic liberal arts college in Michigan, offers choice boards. These boards are structured as charts on which the instructor outlines a variety of assessment options for students to show what they are learning about what is being taught. Charts may include up to nine squares that describe elements the project or product must include to show a student's learning, using the student's preferred medium: drama, graphics, music, multimodals, writing in different genres, and so on.

Options to consider for choices must be based on what you are measuring and what students must show that they have learned from reading and discussing the text. You may invite students to do the following:

- Write a song about the book or choose songs that appropriately reflect key characters
- Film a key scene or a key incident from the book
- Bring in photos of real places or staged scenes that reflect multiple settings or themes
- Create and perform a short reading of a key scene using simple props or costumes or both

The common element in each of these ways of demonstrating understanding is that students must submit on the required due date a written explanation, using specific references or quotations from the beginning, middle, and end of the text, telling why they chose specific music, images, movements, or details. Such assignments may also require a self-reflection that includes a sentence or two in which students state what they learned in preparing this paper, product, or presentation.

The key to designing choice boards is to know what students must demonstrate to you, the teacher, to prove that they understand the concepts and can demonstrate the skills being taught. Offering choice tends to inspire engagement and a desire to complete the task in an admirable way. Further, having students share and show what they are learning further reinforces what you have been teaching. Often students don't "get it" until they see another way of articulating the concept and utilizing the skill.

Consider doing online searches to see ways other educators have incorporated choice boards for assessing reading in college classrooms. Adapt the wording on your own chart to communicate clearly what your students need to include and what you need to see in order for the paper, project, or presentation to earn a passing grade. The general grading guidelines described in chapter 2 usually will suffice for evaluating this kind of student work.

Constructing Found and Pantoum Poems

Invite students to write a found poem. The literary equivalent of a collage, one form of found poetry is often made from newspaper articles, street signs, graffiti, speeches, letters, or even other poems. For an assessment of the novel, students could be required to use specific words and phrases they find in the beginning, middle, and end of the book and arrange these words and phrases into a found but original poem. You could ask them to create four short poems: one each for character, conflict, setting, or for theme.

Students reading *A Day No Pigs Would Die* identify with the boy's physical and emotional growth. They see that he is addressing the same kinds of social fences and facing the same types of adult responsibilities that adolescents must face. After your students finish reading and when you begin discussing the entire book you have been reading together, ask them to capture these themes in a poem using exact words and phrases written by the author. Found poems can also be fun to record in audio and video format and played back to the class, using the principles discussed earlier for digitized presentations.

Another option is for students to write a fourteen-to-sixteen-line poem about the novel you're reading together that portrays incidents, a memorable scene, or a favorite character. They may choose a specific poetic format, one that is structured or unstructured, traditional or new. Your adult students may enjoy writing

- an acrostic,
- a lyric poem,
- a limerick,
- a sonnet,

- a free or blank verse poem,
- a shape poem, or
- a rap.

For these kinds of poems, evaluate the quality based on linguistic precision—vivid verbs and concrete nouns; fresh figurative language—hyperbole, metaphors, similes, symbols, and so on; and, of course, factual accuracy with the novel. Poems can be created individually, in small groups, or even with the entire class. Particularly, with poems using a specific format, you can construct them in real time and project them on-screen. Here is a pantoum poem written collaboratively by a class, as summary and reflection of their reading *Brown Girl Dreaming* by Jacqueline Woodson.

> A girl named Jackie
> In a country divided by race
> Moved from North to south
> Living with the blanket of her grandparent's love
>
> In a country divided by race
> Two siblings and one parent in a long ride "me"
> Living with the blanket of her grandparents' love
> Buried five days a week giving witness to Jehovah
>
> Two siblings and a parent in a long ride "home"
> Anchored in childhood by candy on Friday and ribbons on Sunday
> Buried five days a week giving witness to Jehovah
> Moving gain, New York City, new sibling new life
> A girl named Jackie

CONCLUSION

As you prepare the reading list for your course, check to make sure you have a variety of topics and genres that provide mirrors, windows, and sliding glass doors. This will ensure that your students are learning more about themselves and about the world while they are grappling to achieve the content standards set by your college or department.

Consider ways that fiction written in the twenty-first century fits into a curriculum designed to be student-friendly, culturally relevant to a broad range of students, and also academically vigorous. Adapting ideas from this chapter and using the internet to locate background information for your chosen book helps to enrich your instruction and capture the hopes and fears of your students in much the same way Robert Newton Peck does in his novel about Rob and his pet, Piggy.

With your careful attention, lessons utilizing and building on students' multimedia skills and their multiple-intelligence learning styles provide empowering experiences for you and your students. As traveling companions, you all explore ways that well-told stories can transcend the fences that people put up around themselves and between their communities. With your guidance, your learners discover that contemporary fiction written by diverse authors can help readers erect humane gateways to shared understanding of the diverse experiences that separate and unify us human beings as we seek to live harmoniously in what, at first, was novel territory.

Chapter Five

Developing Critical Thinking While Reading Historical Fiction

I will always be grateful to her for one thing. She taught me my letters. My mistress, I realize now, like many women of her class, had very little education. She read slowly and laboriously, and it always took her several tearful afternoons to compose a letter to her family in Portugal, or to her nephew in Madrid, a young man who was a painter. Yet Mistress had a great deal of practical wisdom, and she knew many things because she trusted her judgment and cultivated her memory.[1]

–*I, Juan de Pareja* by Elizabeth Borton de Treviño

Three sentences. A mistress, an enslaved person, a painter. Tearful afternoons, practical wisdom, and judgment. From Spain to Italy—and beyond. All brought alive through the magic of one work of historical fiction, transporting twenty-first-century readers to Renaissance Europe. Three sentences span thousands of miles and hundreds of years. Here is an entirely engaging education in one novel of historical fiction, thanks to a splendid writer like Borton de Treviño.

Many authors write historical fiction, and this may be a genre on your list to teach. With the ideas here in accessible novels like this one, you can have a great time exploring the past. You will also meet the academic needs of your students and the curriculum standards for your course as you design in-class activities that nurture the ability of your budding scholars to think critically about texts, expand their active vocabulary as they employ the language of literature and rhetoric, and make connections to other times and other peoples.

Not only is teaching historical fiction exciting, but it also is an excellent way to integrate the reading of different genres and texts with other subjects, like social studies, science, and the arts. Like tour companies that include visits to museums or ancient towns as part of their travel packages, you can do the same with your carefully structured lesson planning and use of class time.

Consider collaborating with colleagues in another department. In this case, choose a literary work that introduces or reinforces a historical period or explores some scientific concept your college students are learning in one of those content areas. Such cross-curricular considerations help students see and make connections across disciplines. It also makes for an enriching experience for everyone, instructors and students alike.

ADDING E-BOOKS AS OPTIONS

Since students are required to purchase their own textbooks, for small-group readings, consider books that are available as e-books. The website BuzzFeed News posted "17 Historical Fiction Books That Will Immerse You In A Different Era." Another great source for free e-books is the local public library. An electronic library (MeL) is offered through the Library of Michigan, where students can check out e-books using their library cards. The same may be true in your state. Additionally, Project Gutenberg is an online library of over sixty-thousand titles that users can download or read online for free. More sources include the Internet Archive, Free e-books, Bookbub, and ManyBooks.

After students read short works that introduce the features of the genre, invite students to select one of five titles you have found to be available as e-books. Students then work in small groups to prepare an in-class or multimedia presentation of that text. Select books of comparable length so that most students can complete the book within the time scheduled for the unit of study.

During the unit, allot in-class time for reading and for group meetings. In conjunction with students' reading, you could intersperse mini lessons on the use of and creation of multimedia presentations. In other words, teach students what they need to know about multimedia presentations while they are reading a text of their choice.

USING TEXTS TO INSPIRE A MEDIA PROJECT

A typical one-hour session could incorporate the "I do it, we do it, you do it" mode of classroom instruction.

1. Begin with five minutes of focused writing as an opening activity during which students summarize what they noticed about the most recent reading. For example, you may ask them about the author's use of literary or rhetorical devices or what incidents or claims the students noticed in the text that they know to be true, based on their own experience or observations.
2. Take fifteen to seventeen minutes to present the multimedia task, skill, terminology, or other element that you are teaching. You share the specifics based on the media language and skills your students are required to know and do, such as those you find on media literacy here and in chapter 6.
3. Take five to seven minutes for pairs of students to analyze a sample video that you show. What elements of the structure or strategy you just "taught" do the students see in the sample?
4. Then, allot twenty minutes for students to read silently their chosen text.

Close that segment of the class meeting with students gathering in their chosen book groups to plan ways they will implement what they have just learned and read in the multimedia presentation they will give to the class.

Try it. They will like it.

MAKING CONNECTIONS IN COLLABORATIVE GROUPS

Consider creating a summative assignment in which pairs or small groups create a multimedia presentation in which there is a "Making Connections" component. Students will be required to link current news events to the text on the historical period they are reading. Invite students to brainstorm together or check out today's news issues on a website like Britannica's ProCon.org.

Encourage the group to come to a consensus on one or two issues and show how the main characters in their text are likely to have condemned, condoned, consoled, or counseled someone facing the issue the group has chosen to link to their text. Of course, require that the group cite, in the reference style of your school or college, multiple quotes and specific references from the website and from the beginning, middle, and end of their text to substantiate the claims they make about the character's position on the issue.

WONDERING WHY A PARTICULAR
HISTORICAL NOVEL?

I, Juan de Pareja, by Elizabeth Borton de Treviño, is written as an autobiography from the point of view of Juan, a real African slave inherited by Diego de Velázquez, the court painter for King Philip IV of Spain, who reigned in the seventeenth century. Juan became the assistant of and a friend to Velázquez and, later, an accomplished painter in his own right. One of Juan de Pareja's paintings hangs in the Prado Museum in Madrid, Spain, and Velázquez's painting of Juan is in the New York Metropolitan Museum of Art. See images of both paintings at art sites on the internet.

Books like this may become an immediate favorite to teach if you are inspired by a colleague like Suzanne Federico, who had been "a closet art historian." Federico pointed out that Velázquez's work reflects four schools of European art. Descriptions in the book introduce readers to specific fifteenth- and sixteenth-century painters' artwork and the distinctive characteristics of chiaroscuro, baroque, realism, and idealism.

Borton de Treviño writes so clearly that students hardly realize how much they are learning. But you can ensure that they do so from the very beginning by letting them help build the foundation as they conduct simple research on the historical period and expand their understanding of how to read academic writing.

IMMERSING STUDENTS INTO THE NOVEL

Begin explaining to students the features of historical fiction and that their next class reading will be from this genre. Share with them that historical fiction may include real people, places, and events. Following Louise Rosenblatt's reader-response approach, encourage students to look for the familiar, even in a piece of historical fiction.[2] Remind your adults of a strategy they probably used in their precollegiate days that will serve them well as they begin reading more deeply complex novels in their college classes.

Researching the Historical Setting

The novel, *I, Juan de Pareja*, is set during the Renaissance. In the novel, Rubens (1577–1640), the famous Flemish painter, visits the Spanish court, and Velázquez travels to Italy to purchase art for King Philip. Imagine the budget! As you read this chapter of lessons based on this novel, consider ways you can adapt the activities for a work of historical fiction you are asked to teach. Note places where the descriptions that follow inform, inspire, and intrigue students to read deeply and gain the insight they need to meet course requirements in the class you teach.

The premise of this novel centers on the painting *Las Meniñas*, by Diego Velázquez. This painting, in which Velázquez includes a portrait of himself, has the Cross of Santiago painted onto his garment in an artistic style quite different from his own. Borton de Treviño's tale attempts to explain who painted this cross and why anyone would do so. Consider graphics and include in your teaching slides art and photos that depict the times, places, and events in the work of historical fiction you are teaching.

Cris Tovani, in *I Read It but Don't Get It: Comprehension Strategies for Adolescent Readers*, talks about how reading is thought by many to be simple.[3] Comprehension doesn't happen automatically once you've read the words but, rather, demands complex thinking and connecting new material to what is already known. The more complex the reading, the more it demands of the reader and the more difficult it becomes.

Students who once considered themselves good readers might find themselves frustrated or confused when confronted with difficult selections. Susan Zimmerman and Chryse Hutchins, in *7 Keys to Comprehension: How to Help Your Kids Read It and Get It*, use different terminology but also urge teachers to have students make connections when reading literature.[4] Consider for your adult students the connections these educators advocate in the following relationships:

- Text to self (between the novel and readers' own lives)
- Text to text (among the people, places, and incidents in the novel)
- Text to text (between this and other literature that students have read)
- Text to world (between this book and historical or current events)

If you choose a novel in collaboration with a colleague from another content area, add text to study in history or science or whatever the other content area is. Your adult students will appreciate the fact that you understand that yours is not the only class they will be required to complete in order to earn a degree from an institution of higher learning.

The following discussion uses as a sample historical novel, *I, Juan de Pareja*, by Borton de Treviño, and walks through ways you might design lessons based on the text you assign to your learners. By applying some of the same strategies, you can develop your own approaches to teaching whatever novel you are using.

When you teach a work of historical fiction, it is important to set the scene. Share the work of setting the scene.

Understanding HOW to read different genres is key.
https://www.istockphoto.com/photo/doing-homework-gm515224227-47868696

Presenting Oral Reports Gives an Overview of People and Events

To help set the stage for students to acquire a richer sense of the historical period and to practice their research skills, you can assign students to do research about the real people, places, and events of the period in which the novel is set and to report to the class what they learn.

Use as a guide the facts that may be presented in the book itself. For example, in the foreword of *I, Juan de Pareja*, Borton de Treviño mentions the people of the golden age, such as Galileo, Rembrandt, and Sir Walter Raleigh. Most of the names on this list are so well known that students have little difficulty in locating facts for a brief two-to-three-minute informative speech. The same is likely to be true for the novel you choose since historical novels tend to be written about famous events, well-known places, or legendary people.

Making this an in-class assignment, with small groups working together to find the information and then prepare and present it by the end of the class period, can provide a formative assessment option for you. As you circulate around the room, listening and assisting as needed, you gain insight into the skills the students are acquiring, using, and struggling with. You'll know whether or not further instruction is needed before making this kind of research a homework assignment.

To reduce innocent plagiarism, consider including mini lessons, reviewing how to use websites and programs that check for plagiarism. This mini assignment, which includes conducting simple research, collaborating with peers, practicing speech writing, and giving oral reports, has real purpose.

Check for Gender and Cultural Relevance

As you prep for teaching this novel, you'll see in the foreword of the book, *I, Juan de Pareja,* that many of the names mentioned, such as Galileo, Rubens, and Shakespeare, are familiar, but none are women. However, if you conduct background research on artists of this period, you would learn that two female artists should be included: Artemisia Gentileschi and Elisabetta Sirani.

Both Gentileschi and Sirani were talented artists whose work was equal to that of their male contemporaries. Add their names to your list along with other names of noteworthy women of the Renaissance. If you choose another book and decide to do this assignment, carefully check for and include women of renown from that historical setting and other cultures whose contributions are key to events in that time period. It would make for an interesting mini lesson to discuss with your students both the fact that leaving out female contributions occurs and the reasons for the practice throughout literature.

In days past, it was difficult for students to locate even a little information about women of the Renaissance other than Joan of Arc. However, with ready access to online resources, twenty-first-century students can locate information about Elisabetta Sirani, Artemisia Gentileschi, Grace O'Malley, Christina of Sweden, and Gracia Mendes Nasi, all of whom were active in arts and government during the Renaissance.

For ease in assigning topics, simply have students pull for numbers one through eighteen or more (based on the number of names on the list). Those who have the same number can research the same person and then work together to decide how to make their presentation best. Each presentation should include the following information, based on the five Ws and an H: Who, What, When, Where, Why, and How. Whatever list of people you offer your students, it should reflect both genders as well as cultural, social, economic, and political incidents representative of the historical setting of your book.

Planning for Oral Presentation Based on Renaissance Personages

The following list provides guidance for students' oral presentations:

1. Use an online encyclopedia to discover answers to the following questions for inclusion in your oral report:
   a. Who is the person?
   b. What is this person famous for doing?
   c. When was this person born?
   d. Where was this person born? Locate the country on a world map and include the location in the presentation.
   e. Why is this person's work, invention, discovery, or other accomplishment important in contemporary society?
   f. How was this person's work, invention, discovery, or other accomplishment viewed during this person's lifetime?
2. Keep notes to cite the information that tells where you got your facts. Include the following:
   a. Author of article or entry (if one is listed)
   b. Title of article or encyclopedia entry
   c. Title of encyclopedia or website and its URL
   d. Number of volumes (if applicable)
   e. City where published
   f. Publisher
   g. Year the book was published, article posted, or website updated
   h. Date you accessed the website with information you are using
3. Write a one-page summary that highlights what you learned to make an engaging informative speech. Include a picture, if one is available. (A written summary of 250 words takes about two minutes to speak.)

If your students are tech-savvy and have access to resources at home, consider challenging them to prepare slides for "Pecha Kucha" presentations. These are based on a Japanese concept of using twenty slides, which are advanced every twenty seconds while someone narrates, making a six-minute, forty-second presentation.

For example, you might subdivide the task among four or five groups. Each would be responsible for four or five slides each. Depending on the book you choose, this subdividing could be into categories. For example, for the *Juan* book, the subdivisions could be art, science, math, and religion. Let students decide. Save the slides and show them again before a unit test or semester exam.

Note that this same assignment could be a group in-class task where students do their research together, under your supervision, and polish their work as homework. Groups could meet during the first ten minutes of the next class meeting to review and then present to the class following those refresher meetings. Or, this can be a homework assignment for individual students. You know your students, their access to resources, and the time they really have available for completing this kind of assignment. Design a process through which all can be successful.

You can validate student research by including a question on an end-of-term formal or informal assessment that invites students to share what they learned from their classmates when studying this particular text. You may use a simple question, such as "What are three facts you recall from the presentations your classmates gave when we studied that text of historical fiction?" Doing so validates the work of classmates as they demonstrate on an exam what they have learned during their study of the particular genre.

Creating Symbols to Extend Fact Retention

Symbols and images help students remember details. In their journal section set aside for notes about this historical novel, ask students to create a chart on which they list the names of the historical personages with space to include five Ws and H as well as a column in which to draw symbols or images. During presentations by classmates, have students write down facts that they hear. At the end of the presentations, as you review this information, invite students to recommend appropriate symbols or images to serve as memory aids.

Circulate, observe, and assist as needed.
https://www.istockphoto.com/photo/teacher-helping-young-male-student-in-classroom-gm178462476
  -24524030

For example, for Galileo, someone may suggest a telescope; for Moliere, the happy- and sad-face drama masks; for Isaac Newton, a stick figure sitting under an apple tree; for Joan of Arc, a woman with a sword. Deciding on appropriate symbols is another way to teach to the multiple intelligences your students have; those who learn best by drawing and those who learn best by viewing will benefit from this approach. Consider asking one of the more artistic students to draw the symbols for the class to copy. This can be a fine time for you to stand aside and let them shine.

VARYING ACTIVITIES REINFORCES LEARNING

As an engaging opening activity or an orderly closing to class on days when you have the time, consider projecting slides about the people the class has learned about in their research. One day you could project or show the symbol(s) for ten or more of the historical figures and have students name the person(s) and something for which each is famous. On another day, read the names and ask them to draw the symbol or write a fact about the person. There is no need to collect or grade these quickie quizzes; just conduct "honor" checks. While students are writing their responses, open your grade book and have it ready to record, immediately following the quiz, how they did.

Occasionally, some of your students may extend the assignment on their own and bring in screenshots of articles or ads that either allude to or mention the people on your list or show some symbol of the times. Or you may just ask them to be alert or to do a quick online search of websites to see how many products and companies carry these Renaissance names or to note the names of people or places in the book you are studying. These are just a few ways to have students pay attention to the world around them, think about what they are reading, and contribute to the learning environment they share with you. Do share these ways with your colleagues. Learning with and from others enhances the work of us all.

OFFERING EXTRA CREDIT—YES AND NO

Yes, it is fine to offer extra credit when students find the names of the people mentioned in your text in their history or science texts or in the news they read or view. You want to ensure that students are making connections but not simply finding the names and earning unwarranted extra credit.

To help control dependence on the extra-credit option, limit the percentage of extra points students may earn each marking period to about two or three percent. These extra points can help a student who had a slow start make up for homework points missed earlier in the course or help a student make up for a test or quiz taken when the student was tired, ill, or distracted by some personal issue. With most students, it doesn't take much for them to have an off day!

Extra points, however, should not be so weighty that they make it unnecessary for students to earn passing grades on required curriculum content. Nor should such work take up time students should be giving to learning basic course content or skills. Most important, offering extra-credit points should not require extra work for you, the classroom instructor.

Make your policy on extra-credit work clear at the beginning of the class, both directly and in your syllabus. Consider allowing it only if all required work has been completed. Extra-credit work should be used to boost a grade, not to replace missing assignments.

Extra-credit work should be submitted and recorded at least a week before the last class meeting. The early cut-off date encourages students to monitor their grades throughout the course by checking the online grade book used at your college. Final grades should never be a surprise to anyone. Enforcing this early cut-off date also preserves time for you to grade those assignments needed to determine grades for that course.

WORKING THROUGH THE NOVEL

Consider teaching a historical novel soon after your introductory lessons using short works to review literary terms and rhetorical devices. Adding the historical elements provides a natural reason for doing additional research. By this time, your students have already revived their knowledge of the structure of fiction, more readily recognize the elements of the genre, and remember the literary devices authors use to enhance the storytelling. Your students know how to set up a section in their journal for this new kind of novel and how to write notes as you present facts about the period in which this particular historical text is set. When you begin your unit, just remind students that historical novels are fiction, with plotlines followed in much the same way as short stories.

Your students should also know to pay attention to facts revealed in the exposition, but you may need to review ways to mark their texts or to take notes in their journals. For example, you could have them use a pencil to circle the name of each character when first introduced in the reading. You could have them then underline words or phrases that identify that character. If students are using an electronic version, you could have them highlight and annotate as you have taught for reading and commenting in this virtual environment.

To increase the resale value of their books, some students prefer not to write in their print books. In this case, they can use sticky notes or list names of new characters in their reading journals, including page numbers and a few words or phrases the author uses to identify those characters. Then ask students to remain alert as they continue reading to see if or how the author rounds out the characters through direct and indirect characterization. By this time in their studies, your learners know that the protagonist is a dynamic character, so they are watching to see what encounters bring about the change in this person, from the beginning through the challenge of the conflict and on to the falling action and resolution.

Students can identify the setting by putting a rectangle around words and phrases that indicate time(s) and place(s) or can record this information in their journals. This kind of marking or writing forces students to slow down a bit. It also helps them get to know people and places in the book and, therefore, be less likely to become confused as the action intensifies and conflict complicates. Because *Juan* is written as an autobiography, students quickly notice that the point of view is first person and can predict that the major problem to be solved is one of growing up and surviving the challenges Juan encounters during his lifetime. This may be just the time to share the term *bildungsroman*, the academic term for a "coming-of-age story."

As with all direct instruction of reading, our friend, Carol Jago, reminds educators to help students refine how they examine literature without destroying their confidence as readers. Reminding adults to be active readers increases confidence in their own ability to understand whatever they read, whenever they read, and for whatever purpose they read. Paying attention to the craft and structure of the genre leads students not only toward the curriculum standard goals you are charged to help them reach but also to the reading they do for personal and professional reasons. If students can become known as careful readers, they will be more valuable employees and will be more likely to move up the economic ladder just because they have such skill.

If you are teaching a different historical novel and would like to incorporate a visual-arts component, do so. Historical fiction that works well for this kind of study includes novels your students may have read earlier. If they haven't, do not hesitate to recommend them now. Reading does not have to be hard to read to be useful for teaching and practicing critical reading strategies. A few are listed below.

- *Across Five Aprils*, by Irene Hunt
- *Bud, Not Buddy*, by Christopher Paul Curtis
- *Code Talker: A Novel About the Navajo Marines of World War Two*, by Joseph Bruchac
- *Echo*, by Pam Muñoz Ryan

- *Girl with the Pearl Earring,* by Susan Vreeland
- *Salt to the Sea,* by Ruta Sepetys
- *The Book Thief,* by Markus Zusak
- *Under a Painted Sky,* by Stacey Lee
- *Winterkill,* by Marsha Forchuk Skrypuch

The Library of Congress (LOC) website (loc.gov) and numerous open-access websites provide historical photographs to enhance the study of each of these titles. The LOC site also has sound recordings of real people from American history. Include auditory resources to support students who learn best by listening to real people talk about their lives and times. Hearing these recordings can make these historical personages come alive and be more culturally relevant for all your students. As they read, invite them to bring in photos and graphics they discover along the way. Student contributions help fertilize the garden of your classroom. Their excitement can be the sunshine that helps you all to grow as learners.

Connecting Geography and Map Study

Velázquez and Juan make two trips from Spain to Italy; the story gives their itinerary. Ask students to locate the places on a map and follow the journey by marking the places they visit. Remind students of a book they may have read in middle school, *The Watsons Go to Birmingham,* by Christopher Paul Curtis, which is a fine travel novel written as historical fiction. Sometimes, going back and rereading a book is just the impetus students need to recognize how much they are learning. Having emerging scholars who are adults read "young adult" novels need not be an insult to their intelligence but, rather, a reinforcement of their learning. Invite them to consider sharing the novel with friends and family members using the academic language and knowledge they are now acquiring. How impressive!

Using Google Mapping with Historical Literature

To give students a sense of the realism in fiction, use the Google Maps website to project the following information on the screen:

- Current street-view images of historical sites
- Traditional, satellite-image, and topographical maps of locales
- Website previews of sites about historical buildings, events, and people

For those reading *Juan*, this map work gives students a sense of the distance between towns and the kind of topography the two characters had to cross to get to the Mediterranean Sea and then on to their destinations in Italy. Map reading is a skill most adults are expected to acquire, so asking them to refer to and use maps while studying in your class provides opportunities to practice that skill as they expand their understanding on what is going on in the novel you are reading together. Reading maps also fits with social-justice studies designed to expand students' understanding of others.

Students who are familiar with using satellite-based navigation systems, commonly called "GPS" after the Global Positioning System, will be pleasantly surprised at the information they depend on as they travel. Those who created those resources are likely to have been college students, too. And, just as an aside, a quick internet search will show that it was a Black woman, Gladys West, née Gladys Mae Brown (born October 27, 1930, Sutherland, Virginia), an American mathematician, who is credited with contributing to the development of GPS.

Exploring Friendship: A Multilayered Theme

Elizabeth Borton de Treviño artfully describes friendships between (1) King Phillip and his court painter; (2) the court painter and the enslaved person he owns; (3) the apprentices and an enslaved person; (4) a dwarf and an enslaved person; and (5) a male and a female enslaved person. These relationships are ready-made springboards for discussions about the nature of friendship. In this age of news about intercultural interactions and social justice, getting to know and appreciate others are useful topics to discuss with your college students. As they reflect on their own friendships, your students may be looking in the mirror or looking out the window, learning about others, and gaining insight into the news reports they see on their phones, TVs, and tablets.

You could get the discussion of relationships off the ground by writing the word *friend* in the center of the whiteboard or on something you can project for all to see as you write. Then ask students to brainstorm for words to describe a friend. Without commenting, list their answers around the word "friend," forming a weblike cluster.

Next, ask students to open their journals to the section on this novel, and do a "quick write" on friends or friendships. Set your timer and write along with them, writing nonstop for three or four minutes. Describing their concept or experience with friends usually elicits a level of honesty that may be missing in more prepared writing. They may write about a friendship that went well, one that dissolved, or one they wish existed.

Then invite a few students to read aloud what they have written, respecting their privacy if they decline. Unedited quick writes sometimes reveal emotions too raw to share in public. So, again, honor the choice to pass. While they are writing, if you choose not to write, you could create a word cloud using a free online application. Unfortunately, the very popular word-cloud generator, Wordle.com, was discontinued in 2021, but numerous other apps are available online, including MonkeyLearn, WordItOut, and Jason Davies, to name a few. To create a word cloud, input the terms the students mentioned while brainstorming, and project that computer-generated cloud to summarize your discussion.

Round out the lesson by asking students to write about the friendships they notice are developing in your novel. You may ask them which friendships surprised them and which they think will develop, continue, or end. You may follow up by asking them why and why not. To help students go beyond a simple listing of facts in their speaking and writing, encourage them to continue using "PIE" paragraph format—where they answer the questions by stating their *point (or claim)*, using specific incidents from the text to *illustrate* that point or claim, then *explaining* the reasons they believe the incidents show that the friendship identified begins, continues, or ends.

Because PIE-based writings are more objective than "quick writes," students often are more willing to share them. In fact, some might disagree and even debate their differences about friendship. To keep them focused on the text and to help them practice considering the perspectives of others, challenge them to take an opposing stance they can support with evidence from the book. Doing so, they experience what it is like to give serious consideration to an alternative point of view, which is good practice for developing open minds about others.

Writing about and Discussing Ethical Issues

The issue of ethics, those moral principles that guide our behavior and interaction with others, is one appropriate for discussion in college classes. A unit of study that includes historical fiction, like *I, Juan de Pareja*, provides such opportunities. Juan and the other characters in the book are faced with a number of ethical choices related to slavery, honesty, and loyalty. Consider the presence of ethical issues in the various texts you teach in your class.

The word *ethics* normally refers to defining and using standards of right and wrong, moral and immoral conduct. Ethics also involves analyzing situations in which people have to address moral conduct, duty, and judgment—making right but often tough decisions. Several of the characters in this autobiographical novel are faced with just such choices. As your students read about them, they may identify with these situations even if they disagree with the characters' choices having to do with selling humans as slaves or using mentally and physically challenged persons to entertain the royal children.

Very likely, equally evocative topics will emerge in whatever book you choose to teach. Some raging debates may arise among students when you challenge them to consider the actions and attitudes expressed in the stories they read. Do what you can to monitor but not squelch a heated but respectful exchange of ideas, and let students know that it is perfectly all right to agree to disagree.

RESPONDING HOLISTICALLY TO LITERATURE

Fran Claggett, in *Drawing Your Own Conclusions: Graphic Strategies for Reading, Writing, and Thinking*, wrote that teachers often dissect literature so minutely that students lose sight of the work as a whole.[5] She recommends using art and graphics to give readers an opportunity to "make it whole" again. Here is another opening to assign art, music, or poetry writing for that purpose: to help students reassemble the parts of the story and to see the novel as a whole work of literature.

If you choose to teach historical fiction after exploring reading and writing about the genre of poetry, your students will know that writing can be a poem—even if it does not have a set rhyme or rhythm pattern—as long as the writing "convey[s] a vivid and imaginative sense of experience, especially by the use of condensed language."[6] Invite students to write a pantoum as a summary assignment that pulls together their thinking or experience about the fictional character or events in the book you have just read together.

One assignment is to invite students to compose a narrative poem, similar to a ballad, in which they tell the whole story in quatrains. In this case, have them include at least five, four-line stanzas to account for the exposition, rising action, climax, falling action, and resolution of the story. Hearing alternative views helps to round out and expand the understanding of various genres and texts your adult students study.

ASSIGNING ALTERNATIVE
END-OF-NOVEL ASSESSMENTS

The following are particularly useful kinds of creative, open assignments to offer at the end of a unit. They allow you to see what your students have learned in ways that may not have been revealed in response to earlier assignments. See Stefani Boutelier's choice board idea in chapter 4. Therein, students are invited to choose their own idea, form, or structure to demonstrate what they know. For example, possibilities using the art form of music might include the following:

- Create a melody for each of three or four of the main characters (à la the Darth Vader theme from *Star Wars*)
- Bring in samples of music that reflect three-to-five key scenes (like mood music)
- Bring in three or four different published songs that have lyrics that could have been sung by three or four different characters
- Create original music for any of the three previously mentioned situations

Creative responses might also be from the other art forms of drama, writing, graphic arts, dance, and so on—even cooking. One student made cookies with different spices to represent the personalities of characters in a book we read as a class!

To reinforce the academic standard of giving credit to sources consulted, require students to write a page or two in which they explain the reasons for their choices and to indicate the page(s) of the text that support their choices for music, colors, movements, or spices.

Some college students may complain that you are "dumbing down" the curriculum when you allow students to use artistic projects to show their understanding of the characters, roles, and relationships in the literature. However, after viewing the responses of their classmates, those students will notice and maybe even acknowledge the sophisticated levels of comprehension their classmates' work reflects. These doubters may become so impressed with the depth, breadth, and creativity of their classmates' work that they will try adding art to their own work with more vigor than before.

You can be sure your alternative assignments are well designed and serve as successful alternative assessments if you

- determine in advance what you want to learn about your students,
- tell students the knowledge on which they are being evaluated, and
- give students options to show that knowledge in their dominant intelligence.

Art illuminates
lessons we teach our students
and they understand.

–Anna Roseboro

CONCLUSION

Elizabeth Borton de Treviño's *I, Juan de Pareja* is a rich source of multidisciplinary material for teaching. Reading most historical-fiction texts can provide a luxurious side trip on this college-course journey, the kind one might experience visiting a historical dig while on a trip to the modern high-rise city of Kuala Lumpur. When considering how to approach a work of historical fiction, you could teach it simply as fiction, or you can look at it as a way to have students look at the past in order to see the present and perhaps initiate ways to change the future.

Assignments accompanying this particular book give students opportunities to refine critical reading skills that improve their research skills; hone their speaking abilities; discover Renaissance people, places, and events; view art by renowned painters; and write about and discuss issues of friendship and ethics. Adapting the plans offered in this chapter will empower you and your students to meet the majority of the end-of-course standards set for the course you are teaching, and you all will be learning.

Like the mistress described in *I, Juan de Pareja*, your students may at first find that they read slowly and laboriously and have to spend tearful afternoons writing. But, once they have the pleasure of getting to know about people and places, delving into another time period through reading, writing, viewing, and discussing ideas to which they can relate today, they will feel more confident and competent in demonstrating their refined language and rhetorical skills and in meeting the personal challenges they face in the century in which they live.

Chapter Six

Reading Essays, Speeches, and the Media

If you are like English language-arts educators from the middle of the twentieth century, you may have yet to consider nonfiction when you began thinking about teaching genres. Back then, genres were more often referred to as fictional literature, and literature is what one taught in English classes. What is ironic about how we studied fiction, poetry, and drama is that most students were asked to write nonfiction essays in response to that literature.

However, as that century wound down and the twenty-first century began, more and more educators recognized nonfiction as a legitimate genre with powerful uses and purposes to describe, explain, convince, and more. They began to see the value of teaching students how to read and write essays, how to write and present their thinking as public speeches, and how to share what they were learning in mediums using various electronic devices. These changes in perspective, along with the explosion of virtual communications and social media has made understanding how both nonfiction and media is used a critical component of reading instruction in college courses.

This chapter demonstrates ways to build lessons into your course that will have students learning the language of nonfiction, and also reading and analyzing essays, speeches, and media, thus better understanding the unique traits of yet another broad genre, nonfiction, and three of its subcategories.

EXPLORING THE ESSAY

"Essays are a short literary composition that reflects the author's outlook or point. A short literary composition on a particular theme or subject, usually in prose and generally analytic, speculative, or interpretative."[1]

The term "essay" comes from the French verb "essayer" meaning "to try." Originally, this descriptor for nonfiction referred to writers' attempts to articulate their thoughts on specific topics. As the printing press made writing more widely accessible to the public, more and more people began writing and publishing their thoughts on topics including politics, religion, and science. More and more schools found that textbooks could be printed and distributed for student use as a supplement to the lecturing that had occurred in prominent colleges and universities.

Over time, recurring traits began to appear in this writing, and the public began to expect these essays to reflect specific structural features and patterns of organization. Just as genres of fiction have unique qualities that differentiate them from one another, nonfiction essays, speeches, and the media have their own set of literary terminology. You may recognize these as rhetorical devices, text structures, and traits of public speaking. More recently added is the grammar of media, which usually refers to messaging that uses visual images, movement, and color. These components are manipulated in different ways to achieve specific purposes in communicating with identifiable audiences.

Reading Academic Essays

Students are often expected to read numerous forms of essays, but little instruction is given on how to read them effectively. People read and write a variety of essays in daily life without recognizing them as a distinctive genre, but schools focus primarily on what is referred to as the academic essay. Scholarly writing is most often based on research collected through either primary or secondary methods.

The academic essay is the most formal of the genre, and the expository essay is the one most frequently used in schools, often in response to literature. Students are frequently asked to analyze or compare and contrast using the ubiquitous five-paragraph format. However, other types of essays include descriptive, narrative, persuasive (sometimes called problem/solution), and argumentative. These more purposeful forms are used throughout everyday life in editorials, letters to the editor, debates, blogs, letters of complaint, and so on. Most often students are taught about these forms and asked to use them in writing or speaking. However, when the focus is on reading essays, teachers often make the assignment to read and leave students to navigate on their own.

Few of our adult college students have had high-school teachers like Sarah Hahn Campbell, who recounted her conversation with a student in a recent *English Journal* article:

> "I don't understand this scholarship prompt," Aamiina complained, slumping down into the seat beside me (names are pseudonyms). She adjusted her hijab.

I leaned over to look at her computer screen and read for a moment. "They just want you to explain your personal feelings about all the states trying to pass laws against discussing race and racism in schools."

Aamiina frowned. "But that's what I don't get. You give us all these examples of beautiful writing, but I don't know how to discuss ideas."[2]

When lessons suddenly became stale, Campbell realized that she had been teaching her students to approach research in a way that "had not required them to wrestle with the world." Campbell took a chance and abruptly changed the focus of her research class in a way that energized her teaching and her students with an approach that allowed them to engage in the joy of learning. She reinserted the role of student voice and allowed the research to be driven by the students themselves.

Preparing students to read essays effectively involves using many of the same strategies used for previewing textbooks and novels, described in chapter 4 and elsewhere in this book. Begin with an overview with the rhetorical analysis questions shared by Jim Burke and Kia Richmond.

Unlocking the Research Essay

Some new-to-college students are stumped, even stunned, when while doing their own research, they come across academic essays written by an expert on the student's chosen topic. The author's sentence structure may be difficult to understand and the academic vocabulary and terminology unfamiliar. Reduce student resistance to keep reading by designing an in-class lesson that identifies the distinctive components of this genre of nonfiction. You can make it personal by sharing excerpts from your own thesis or academic writing or sharing on a topic about which your students already have expressed interest.

As your students come to understand the purpose and audience for this genre of text, they are more likely to recognize the WHYs and HOWs of the contents in the introduction, body, and conclusion. Share with them that research writing is designed (1) to credit those who've come before, (2) to rationalize the reason for the research, (3) to describe the process of gathering data, (4) to analyze and reflect on what has been learned doing the research, and often concludes with (5) a call for action, to continue the research or to utilize the findings in the field. When students notice the elevated language, specific topic jargon, and longer sentences, they are reminded that the audience often includes those already familiar with the subject or interested in learning more.

Numerous online resources are available with strategies for reading academic writing and for evaluating sources. The writing centers at George Mason University and the University of North Carolina both address these strategies.

Having Read It, Should They Use It?

Most college teachers assign reading for information or as models for writing on topics related to their course or of interest to their students. To support their claims, students are often asked to include or to provide information from outside, reliable sources. So, the logical next step is to use in-class time for direct instruction on evaluating sources. Ask your learners to locate and consider answers to these questions:

1. Who is the author? What are the author's credentials? Is the author considered to be an expert in the field? What are the author's affiliations?
2. Who published the information? Is the publisher a reliable source? What is the domain extension: .com or .edu?
3. When was the information published? Is it current or is it considered to be a "classic" source? Is it a standard source?

As you flesh out your lessons, refer to quality online sources for additional information on evaluating sources. A fun one to start with may be the CRAAP Test developed by Sarah Kurpiel at Benedictine University Library.

Considering Satire about Formulaic Writing

Mara Lee Grayson, an associate professor of English and a specialist in composition and rhetoric and teacher education at California State University, Dominguez Hills, located in the South Bay region of Los Angeles, offers this strategy to spark thinking about formulaic writing. She teaches literature and rhetoric and composition to adult students who are predominantly Chicanx/Latinx or Black/African American. Grayson says:

> I almost invariably share with students at some point in the semester, composition scholar Edward M. White's "My Five-Paragraph-Theme Theme." Instead of giving students the full version of the essay, which includes White's commentary, I give them only what he calls the "jeu d'esprit" with which he opens. For those unfamiliar with the essay, the satirical opener, credited to "Ed White," is composed of five short, vague paragraphs true to the form of the five-paragraph essay that is the subject of the satire.
>
> Without citing existing scholarship or crafting an overt critique, White makes readily apparent the shortcomings of formulaic writing instruction and assignments by writing a five-paragraph essay lauding the five-paragraph essay form with faint praise like it "keeps you from thinking too much, which is a great time saver, especially on an essay test."

After reading the excerpt, Grayson says, the students generally agree with what has been written because their professor has spent valuable class time reading and talking about it. But some wonder. Few, however, challenge the writing. Reading the piece, they may have a nagging suspicion about the tone they've picked up on, but they aren't sure, so, in class they stay quiet. They don't want to be wrong. They know something is strange, off, doesn't feel right.

Yet new-to-college students may assume that the text is what it purports to be, and that academic writing means what it says. They assume that scholarly writing and other nonfiction writing aren't humorous, sarcastic, or satirical. They've been taught the five-paragraph theme so many times they think it actually is best practice, despite decades of composition scholarship that says otherwise. Students who are also educators may have even been taught to teach it in their own classrooms or to students they tutor. And even if they disagree with the praise awarded to the five-paragraph format, they assume that their professor would not give them a text she didn't agree with.

This strategy of using satire may be ticklish but consider it as you reflect and explore the genre of satire while expanding students' understanding of the need to validate the author, purpose, and message of what they read.

Noting Peritext in Textbooks

Your students may recognize some of these supplemental text features in expository nonfiction works and may need to be reminded of ways these features work in their textbooks and on websites. In that first case, readers are paying attention to chapter titles, images that may be added to certain pages, diagrams, maps, charts, or unexpected spacing that sometimes also appears in fiction. Chapter titles often signal what is to come.

Your students may have noticed that authors of modern fiction sometimes choose to write from multiple points of view, and the only clue to changes in viewpoint may be an extra space between paragraphs or a flourish or line to indicate this shift in perspective. Students may be confused if they miss these delicate peritext cues. These subtle cues sometimes are used in nonfiction, too.

Learning to Use Text Structure

If text structures are not defined or explained in your course text, several websites include definitions and mini lessons to help you get started. Most suggest that teachers do the following:

- Introduce the idea that expository texts have a text structure
- Introduce common text structures: sequence/chronological order, classification, definition, process, description, comparison, problem/solution, cause/effect
- Show examples of paragraphs that correspond to each text structure
- Examine topic sentences that provide a clue to the reader about the text's specific structure
- Model the writing of a paragraph that uses a specific structure
- Have students try writing paragraphs that follow a specified structure
- Have students read their peers' drafts and give oral or written feedback

For students who are proficient with paragraph organization, do the last three steps (above) with longer chunks of text or entire chapters, as suggested by the National Education Association.

Students often miss the signal words or transitions that help them process the ideas presented in essays, so reviewing those is helpful, too. The internet is an excellent resource for fleshing out your lists of signal words based on the prior knowledge, skills, cultures, and needs of your students. There you will find appropriate charts that include such words and phrases as *for example, first, then, furthermore, on the other hand, consequently, finally,* and so on. Once you get them started, students can skim through their books and find examples of more words to add to your list.

Remember from your study of poetry that poetry is someone saying something to someone? That's the case with essays, too. As you teach your students to read and understand essays, have them seek to discover who is speaking; for what general purpose (to inform, argue, persuade, entertain, or commemorate); with what message; and to what audience. Additional questions that students should address are "How does the writer organize the essay to achieve that purpose?" and "What rhetorical devices has the author employed for that audience?"

UNDERSTANDING THE ROLE OF VALUES

An exercise that helps students consider purpose and audience has them look at values. Yes, by carefully inspecting word choice, sentence syntax, and organization, readers can discover what is important to the researcher or essay writer. Readers can get a hint of what the audience thinks is important, too. Your question to them is "How do you, the reader know?" For the most part, any answer students can validate or support with evidence from the text with logical reasons should be accepted. This is where using the "PIE" structures

Misunderstanding values leads to misunderstanding messages and messengers.
https://www.istockphoto.com/photo/two-angry-students-looking-each-other-with-hate-gm950676344
  -259494582

discussed in chapters 2 and 4 helps reduce arguments among students who may disagree. When they state their position (claim), illustrate it with examples, and explain the connection between the two, let it go.

As students mature and become more informed and perceptive about social issues, they become more alert to the fact that the context of writing is key to understanding the message. One approach to making this point is inviting students to consider the "SEPSs" of fiction or nonfiction texts.

SEP refers to the social, economic, and political climate of the times in which the writing was published. Examining the SEPs means asking the following questions:

1. How might the text have been perceived by readers of that era?
2. Who is the author of the text?
3. When, historically, was it written?
4. Where (city, town, country) was it written?
5. What was going on at the time?

Answers to questions like this often are found in the opening sections of academic writing because researchers know that such "climate" influences the writer and the message.

Revealing Values

Prepare your students to read more deeply, gaining more insight from fewer readings. Step back for a moment before you have them analyzing articles, reading and listening to speeches, or viewing video and media about controversial issues. Develop a short presentation on values. This is an opportunity for your learners to contemplate what we humans think is important to ourselves, for us, and for those we care about. What influences our behavior and colors our lenses when we read, listen, and view communication in any form?

This activity can clarify, without being too cynical, that "shared values" is an amorphous and ever-changing concept. The following word-cloud activity shows this specifically. There will be several values that most students agree on; there will also be some less broadly shared values. It would be interesting to see how your learners respond. How would you, the teacher, feel if five of your top ten core values did not get magnified?

Here is a concise lesson during which you and your class create a word cloud:

1. Distribute a list of forty to fifty words you compile when searching online for core values.
2. Ask students to circle ten words that represent what they value.
3. Redistribute these anonymous lists to students on opposite sides of the room (left side gets right side's lists and vice-versa).
4. Have students read that list aloud while one volunteer (a student who word processes accurately and speedily) enters all the words as they are read. Repetition is fine. The number of times a word appears on the final list will determine the size in which the word will appear in the word cloud. Consider using the talk-to-text feature in your word processing application, like those found in MS Word and Google Docs.
5. Copy and paste the class list of value words into an online app that generates word clouds. The resulting word cloud will show explicitly the primary values of your class. Consider free online word-cloud generators like https://www.wordclouds.com/, https://monkeylearn.com/word-cloud/, or https://www.mentimeter.com/features/word-cloud.
6. Project the word cloud without comment. Allow students to view it for a full sixty seconds before discussing their class cloud of values with each other.

It will be enlightening for your students to see the range of values held among their peers. After hearing and seeing what the class believes is important, the students will have a common language to write and talk about these controversial topics. Your students may find it interesting to read pro/con essays found on this website: http://www.procon.org/. Often when students see these kinds of differences, they can understand why intelligent, thoughtful people disagree on topics important to them all.

Then, using that same list of value words, ask students to consider what they think writers of the articles and speeches and creators of media value. Ask the class members to point out words, phrases, images, what is missing, who is quoted, and so on. Equally informative for readers is thinking about what the target audience values and ways the writer or creator recognizes and appeals to those values.

This lesson on discovering values works well with one described in chapter 2 on responding to literature, "Nine Yardsticks," which is a structured way to look at, evaluate, and critique literature. One of the yardsticks is *personal beliefs*; in using this yardstick, the student considers the fact that personal beliefs determine how readers respond to what they read, hear, and view.

Reading Persuasive Essays and Speeches

Providing probing questions helps students to read essays and speeches and, eventually, to apply similar strategies when writing their own ideas to publish or present in person or online. For example, if you assign students to read an essay or speech to persuade, remind them that most persuasive writing

Nine YARDSTICKS of Value

Yardstick	1	2	3	4	5
Clarity					
Escape					
Reflection					
Artistry					
Internal Consistency					
Tone					
Emotional					
Personal Significance					

Chart evaluations as a prewriting strategy.
Chart from *More about Writing* (2019), p. 80

includes information for the audience to learn, arguments to make them contemplate, and calls for actions to persuade them to change their thinking or behavior. Then, have pairs of students read the sample text to determine the kinds of arguments they notice.

1. Does this writer make appeals to the *head* (definitions, statistics, explanations, and comparison/contrast)?
2. Does this writer make appeals to the *heart* (humor, explanation, illustrations, quotations, testimony, or stories about real people)?
3. Does this writer make appeals to the *pocket* (definitions, facts, statistics, and comparison/contrast related to money)? This appeal is sometimes combined with the first.

You may recall these in a more formal light as Aristotle's rhetorical devices of *ethos*, *logos*, and *pathos*. Go ahead and introduce this vocabulary to discuss argumentation and persuasion. Your students are likely to see use or allusions in their research for your class and other college courses.

Compelling Arguments

Appeal to head...

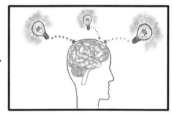

...heart...

...and pocket.

Persuasive arguments may appeal to the head, heart, and pocket.
Chart from *More about Writing* (2019), p. 84

When your students write, insist that they use ethical arguments that do not devolve into use of fallacies they see in some commercials and political rantings, such as:

- Ad hominem fallacy
- Appeal to ignorance
- Band wagoning
- Circular argument
- False dilemma/false dichotomy
- Hasty generalization
- Red herring
- Slippery slope
- Straw man

Online websites have public-domain graphics that visually, sometimes humorously, show what each of these fallacies looks like and thus clarify for your students the use of the ways some writers, speakers, and makers of film create compelling communication.

Jim Burke, who has taught high-school and community-college students in the Bay Area of California, offered tips in an online presentation, "Teaching Academic Essentials."[3] He urges educators to provide students with dependable, transferable tools for reading, writing, thinking, and participating in the real world. For example, a writer may assert and argue but not conclude. A writer may mention but not include a call for action. To help get students started choosing specific verbs about ways ideas are presented in essays, Burke provides this list of such verbs for students to consider as they compose their position sentences or thesis statements:

- Argues
- Asserts
- Concludes
- Considers
- Discusses
- Emphasizes
- Examines
- Explores
- Focuses on
- Implies
- Mentions
- Notes
- Points out
- Says

- States
- Suggests

Prior to giving Burke's assignment, spend some in-class time having your student writers check the definition of the terms in the suggested list and choose the word that has both the denotation and connotation they wish to convey in their writing.

GIVING AN ORAL REPORT OR
PRESENTING A SPEECH?

Are you one of the college instructors or professors who bemoans the fact that you find it a challenge to teach students to give a "good" speech? Like other colleagues in your department, do you acknowledge that students do well on "oral reports," yet something still is lacking? Speech giving really is different from giving an oral report. But how?

Ask your students a few questions, and the features become clear. Start your unit on reading and presenting public speeches by asking your savvy students what they notice about a good speaker. Surprisingly, they seldom comment on the content of the speech, but instead point out aspects of delivery like giving verbal clues to organization patterns, making eye contact, using gestures, rate of speaking, clear articulation, varied intonation, poise, and so on. Of course, your current students may not use these terms, but what they mention shows clearly that *how* the report is delivered is the key feature that makes the speech an effective one.

Therefore, if you expect your students to become effective, competent, and confident speakers, it seems only right that you incorporate into your lesson planning opportunities for students to observe and critique good speaking and also the time to write and practice their own speeches. Ask them to watch television news reporters. Find and show them short video clips of politicians, businesspeople, or community members delivering speeches. Watch an inspirational speaker giving a talk. Websites such as TED Talks include presentations on a range of topics by an even wider range of speakers. Try Taylor Mali's TED talk on "What Teachers Make." With careful screening, you will find videos with diverse speakers that can inform and inspire your emerging speakers.

Urge your students to watch the speakers they see and hear regularly. Encourage them to reflect on or pay attention to the delivery styles of their imams, pastors, priests, and rabbis. After just a few observations, your student monitors can assemble a list of those characteristics of content, structure, style, and vocal qualities that make oral presentations simple to follow and easy to remember. Next, encourage students to pattern effective deliveries that fit their own personal style.

PRESENTING A SPEECH

Giving a speech is more than reading an essay aloud. An effective speech is both an oral and a visual presentation designed for a specific audience in a specific place for a specific purpose. Since public speaking is designed to be heard, few listeners come prepared to take notes. They will retain more of what they hear if the content and delivery are designed to help listeners know what to listen for and provide spoken cues to remind them of what they have heard. Effective speakers dress for the occasion and use voice and physical qualities to enhance what is being said.

During your study of the text of speeches, students probably recognize that speech writers include more repetition to guide the audience in following, comprehending, and recalling ideas presented. The students notice the use of shorter, more declarative sentences comprised of vivid verbs, concrete nouns, and graphic images. Speech writers carefully incorporate vocabulary chosen for its sound and suggestive power. Sound familiar? Sounds like poetry, doesn't it?

By this time, your students also will point out that carefully chosen transitions help hold the speech together while keeping the listeners on track with the positions, arguments, and stories being presented through informative, persuasive, and entertaining speeches. These transitions often are the same signal words learned in your teaching of text structure in essays. Take note, instructors: Your students are noticing the similarities in the various genres of literature—even those they are being taught as distinctive kinds of writing.

A thoughtful speaker takes into consideration what the audience sees as it listens. This begins with attire, gestures, and the use of physical space. The speakers also practice their oral presentation often enough to be able to deliver it at a pace that is easy to follow, using pauses, pacing, and volume to attract and retain attention throughout the speech. Consider showing videos of short speeches to demonstrate these distinguishing traits of a public speech versus the oral reading of an essay. But, after the first minute, turn off the volume and let students just watch the speaker for a couple of minutes before raising the volume again. Students will quickly get the point.

Speaking for Different Purposes

Generally, there are four basic kinds of speeches, and during the weeks of your course you can ask students to read, then prepare and present one of each: to inform, to persuade, to entertain, and to commemorate. None need be long; all must be purposeful. And you do not have to wait until later in the course to have a formal speech unit of two or three weeks, assignments for analysis of speeches, and the time to complete their presentations. While elements of preparation and practice both are keys to effective public presentations, having given informal speeches throughout the course, students have personal experience to reflect upon should you begin direct instruction about public speaking.

Picking a Topic and Planning a Speech

For your adult students, consider designing a news-related speech assignment where students are asked to think critically about authentic purposes for persuasive speaking and then to conduct research, use correct citation and documentation, and finally write and present a speech on a current issue. In this case, too, you can link the assignment to a text you are studying.

You may, for example, have assigned a lesson for which students select a news-related topic that might interest one of the characters from a novel or article the class has read or is studying. Or, you may have them write and present a speech to address a problem at the college or in their current or home community (problem/solution). Students generally respond enthusiastically and are willing to practice their newly developing skills when they are allowed to apply these skills to a social-justice topic that is important to them. Offer students the option of giving the speech in the persona of a fictional character. Doing so provides reluctant students a safe mask and some distance between a controversial topic and their class as an audience.

Playing to the Audience

We may giggle when thinking of this expression, but the nature of the audience is a vital consideration when planning any kind of communication. José Luis Cano, when teaching at a predominantly Latinx community college in Brownsville, Texas, taught the value of audience in culturally sensitive ways. While the school doesn't keep statistics of students who speak bilingually, a quick walk-through of the institution reveals its presence. The "Composition I" course held an explicit outcome that focused on edited American English, but the "Composition II" course leaned heavily toward rhetorical theory. Consequently, in the "Composition II" course, Cano made use of the rhetorical concept of "audience" as one of the assessments.

For this assignment, Cano invoked a bilingual audience through the construction of a poster with a *refrán/dicho* (proverb/words of wisdom). He assigned this project toward the end of the semester because, by that time, students had built a familiarity with concepts in rhetorical theory, and they were used to discussing certain terms, namely "audience." As an educator, he chose this particular assignment because it made use of a linguistic dexterity that most students possess and imagines an entirely different audience than an academic one. Students who felt uncomfortable could still create the poster in English only.

Being aware that thoughtful authors often demonstrate rhetorical bilingualism in their writing should not surprise college students. As they read and note that some authors include regional slang, like that from Appalachia, or "Spanglish" (a mix of Spanish and English sometimes heard in the southern border states). One may see "Frenchlish," which is the Franco-English employed for readers along the northern borders of the United States, and versions of urban slang distinctive to cities across the nation.

Doing It Wrong to Make It Right?

An adjunct professor in the writing department at Grand Valley State University, Roz Roseboro has a variety of students who are about the same age, and most are residents of Michigan. However, they come with a range of precollegiate experiences, and some are shyer than others. About midsemester, prior to assigning the first oral presentation for which the students will be graded, she recommends playing "Eli's game." By this time in the term, the learners have developed a sense of community and likely are ready to ham it up for their small group, illustrating what it looks and sounds like to be a bad speaker.

While a member of the same cohort of graduate teaching assistants at Northern Michigan University (NMU), Elijah Sparkman, currently a Michigan teaching artist, told Roseboro about a game he had learned from Nancy Gold, a contingent associate professor at NMU. Professor Gold encouraged the cohort members to share these at NMU, and they continue to do that now as we two are doing in this book.

Roseboro found what she now called "Eli's Game" worked well at NMU, and she has incorporated into class activities this strategy for prepping students to give oral presentations based on their writing. For the game, use index cards as playing cards on which you write an attribute or action for the students to consider. Note in the bulleted list that follows the nine auditory qualities and observable body language. Have enough sets of cards for groups of four-to-six students.

Roseboro uses game pieces and dice she bought online, but you could just as easily use a coin or something else as a token and a dice generator application on someone's phone.

As students arrive on the day you plan to do this activity, or during their break between class sessions, have students write on the board a short list of topics they could talk about with no preparation. Topics could be how to do something or why they like or dislike something (e.g., how to make an omelet, why the Bears are always terrible, the first time I drove on the highway—low stakes stuff!)

The gameplay is simple:

1. Arrange the index cards in a circle.
2. Place the game piece or token on any card.
3. The first student rolls the die and moves the game piece enough times to match the number on the dice.
4. The group picks a topic from the whiteboard and that first person must stand up (and standing up IS important) and talk about that topic for thirty seconds while demonstrating their choice of what is on the card.
   a. Hands: Move your hands or don't move them at all while you talk.
   b. Mumble: Mumble or speak with exaggerated diction.
   c. Monotone: Speak in a monotone or with exaggerated up and down tones.
   d. Constant: Talk for the whole thirty seconds.
   e. Speed: Talk really fast or talk really slow.
   f. Posture: Stand with excellent or terrible posture.
   g. "Like": Say "like" a lot or try not to say it at all.
   h. Eye Contact: Make or don't make any eye contact as you talk.
   i. Audience: The group gets to decide who the audience is for your talk (e.g., senior citizens, kids, or people who speak another language).

In a twenty-minute chunk of class time, each student should be able to stand and deliver three or four times to his or her group. The outgoing students usually ham it up. The quieter ones almost always crack a smile, but they know all must participate, and they do.

Roseboro acknowledges that she doesn't have her students do a presentation prior to this game, so it's difficult to quantify how effective it is. But, she concludes, "What I can say is that I rarely see students mumbling, standing with poor posture, or moving their hands excessively when they do present, for a grade. Moreover, I do find students commenting on some of these attributes in their peer reviews."

Note the ways that this opportunity to do it wrong can draw your learners' attention to what makes an effective oral presentation while they are playing a game. Doing it wrong can teach students to do it right. See the chart for scheduling a week of speeches later in this chapter.

Students will be empowered for life. As they continue their education and transfer their learning to the world of work, students you teach are not likely to be passed up for a job promotion simply because they lack the reading, speaking, and media skills called for in most collegiate coursework and sought in twenty-first-century job markets.

Getting Off to a Good Start and Using a Variety of Evidence

As students peruse published speeches and then pattern them for speeches of their own, have them ask questions like those that follow to discover what makes the persuasive speech they read effective and the speech the student is writing equally so.

1. Does this speech open with an attention-getter that makes the audience want to listen? A question, a startling fact, a quote—using one of these to start an essay immediately grabs readers' attention.
2. Does the introduction include *signposts* or *signal words* that indicate the order of the arguments to follow?
3. Does this speech clearly show that this topic is important to the speaker (personally or as the character)?
4. Does this speech clearly show why this topic is important to the members of the real or fictional audience? Consider known or assumed values.
5. Does this speech provide adequate support for each main section of the speech? Check the number of times the speech writer includes each of these supporting elements in the speech:

_____ Illustrations/examples		_____ Explanations	
_____ Definitions		_____ Restatements	
_____ Statistics/numbers		_____ Humor	
_____ Comparison/contrast		_____ Opinion of experts	
_____ Testimony		_____ Quotations	

Having the students make a script of their speech is a practical way to have them practice the grammar of Standard English they have been learning, too. If, however, it is appropriate for their speech to be in another version of English, encourage them to use it. The goal is to communicate clearly both in writing and speaking in an appropriate grammar, whether it is the grammar of Standard English or another.

Speakers' choice of grammar makes a difference in how well they get their ideas across to their audience, even if their purpose is to entertain peers in their class by commemorating a character in a story, a historical figure in history, or a real friend or family member. If they choose not to use Standard English, ask them to articulate why the language they choose is appropriate for their purpose and audience. That is what Cano illustrates in his rhetorical bilingualism assignment, as described earlier.

Practicing, Practicing, Practicing

Insist that your students get feedback on their speeches before presenting them in class for evaluation. This listener could be a friend, a family member, a lodger in the student's dorm, or a classmate in another course. Practicing aloud is the only way for students to know for certain they are familiar enough with the content of their speech to deliver it with confidence while making eye contact, using gestures, pronouncing words correctly and clearly, varying the pace of the speaking, and maintaining their poise.

Students sometimes wonder what they should be paying attention to when they practice a speech, so plan on providing a few guidelines to assure these soon-to-be speakers that they are on the right track. Strongly suggest that they time themselves as they give their speech at least three times standing in front of a mirror, holding their notes on the same index cards, tablet, or cell phone they plan to use when they give their speech in public. If they can look up at themselves and keep talking through their speech, they probably are prepared to look up and make more frequent eye contact with their audience.

Share with the student speakers the criteria on which their oral presentations will be assessed, such as *content, organization, vocal issues,* and *appearance.* See the chart titled "SPEECH Schedule by COLOR GROUPS" for organizing a series of speeches with students in color groups of four to five students, who write peer feedback on one trait during each class meeting, except the day or portion of the class when their color group is presenting. This structure also works well for other kinds of in-class presentations of projects. If your class meets for more than an hour at a time, remember to include a short break between rounds of speeches.

Encourage your students to dress appropriately on the day they give the speech, perhaps in an outfit that is neat, comfortable, and appropriate for their intended audience. Choosing what to wear reminds them that people in an audience are spectators who are influenced by the speaker's physical appearance and posture. Thoughtful speakers want audiences to pay attention to what they say and not be distracted by their attire, hair, or jewelry. When resources are available at home or at school, recommend that your students make an audio or video recording and listen and watch to hear and see what others are to hear and see when the students deliver their speeches. Cell phones are perfect for this.

SPEECH Schedule by COLOR GROUPS

Day	RED	GREEN	PURPLE	ORANGE	BLUE
1	*SPEAKING* (no feedback)	Comment on CONTENT (appropriate for the audience, variety of support, appeals, quality of evidence, sources cited, etc.)	Comment on ORGANIZATION (introduction with SIGNPOST (statement of PURPOSE) TRANSITIONS (appropriate for kind of speech) and CONCLUSION (summary, reflection, or reflection without introducing new ideas)	Comment on VOCAL ISSUES (articulation, intonation, pace, pauses, volume, etc.)	Comment on APPEARANCE (appropriate gestures, use of visuals, aids of physical space)
2	APPEARANCE	*SPEAKING*	CONTENT	ORGANIZATION	VOCAL ISSUES
3	VOCAL ISSUES	APPEARANCE	*SPEAKING*	CONTENT	ORGANIZATION
4	ORGANIZATION	VOCAL ISSUES	APPEARANCE	*SPEAKING*	CONTENT
5	CONTENT	ORGANIZATION	VOCAL ISSUES	APPEARANCE	*SPEAKING*

When students are asked to give a little more attention to observing and to recognizing the qualities of a good speech and are given time to research, write, and practice, students become attuned to differences in effectiveness. These emerging communicators no longer will be content simply to give a well-written report but will endeavor to present an engaging speech.

LEARNING MEDIA GRAMMAR

For decades, English language-arts educators have taught students the grammar rules for writing and the grammar rules of literature (plot structure for fiction and text structure for nonfiction) but only recently have begun to teach the grammar of media. Twenty-first-century students view other print and electronic media many more hours per day than they read traditional books. For this reason, we are beginning to see media literacy included among the standards you are expected to teach in general-education courses across the content areas. The College and Career Readiness Anchor Standards for Speaking and Listening call for all curricula to include assessments to determine how well students can "[i]ntegrate and evaluate information presented in diverse media and formats, including visually, quantitatively, and orally."[4]

Knowing media grammar leads to critical viewing.

https://www.istockphoto.com/photo/watching-tv-series-at-home-gm543590716-97581329

You can design lessons to teach your students how to "read the media" found in magazines and film as well as on websites.

Lots of internet resources are found on such sites as NCTE's ReadWriteThink.org, National Writing Project, and Edutopia.org, and some include interviews about the value of teaching the grammar of media literacy and a variety of video clips to use for classroom instruction. The ReadWriteThink website has a specific section on media literacy that includes actual lesson plans. Or you can just use magazines you collect and invite students to bring to class or digital files of images you compile and project in electronic slide programs like PowerPoint or Google Slides.

Some simple lessons introduce the students to the use of color and layout. Other more in-depth lessons may involve learning the language of film— camera angles, use of lighting, timing of shots, and numbers of cuts—and then viewing samples alone and then in groups. Consider in-class activities for which small groups of students create short videos or webpages that illustrate the concepts you are teaching.

Deconstructing the Grammar of Media

Students as digital consumers need to recognize that not everything on the internet is true and objective. Becoming a critical and effective reader in this relatively new medium includes several stages:

- Viewing
- Assessing source reliability
- Creating their own
- Viewing and critiquing
- Deconstruction to determine what worked

A collection of lesson plans developed by the Center for Media Literacy (CML) includes "Five Key Questions" and "Five Core Concepts."[5]

Five Key Questions

1. Who created this message?
2. What creative techniques are used to attract my attention?
3. How might different people understand this message differently?
4. What values, lifestyles, and points of view are represented in, or omitted from, this message?
5. Why is this message being sent?

Five Core Concepts

1. All media messages are constructed.
2. Media messages are constructed using a creative language with its own rules.
3. Different people experience the same media message differently.
4. Media have embedded values and points of view.
5. Most media messages are organized to gain profit or power or both.

Becoming a critical viewer is just the first step in learning how to read the media. Producing that media is the step that shows that learning is taking place.

Assessing News Grammar

This news-related assignment requires students to conduct research, practice citation and documentation, and think more critically about persuasive techniques. During the first two weeks of this month-long assignment that can be combined with a fiction unit, students are to select a topic reported in a print or digital medium. Then bring in copies of four or five written articles relating to that topic; they can also use text transcriptions of television reports that are available on local and network websites. If your students have access to the internet, they can follow the news easily. The purpose is to have them follow the news for a month, paying attention to stories on their chosen topics. They then can prepare to assess ways the nonfiction writing is the same as and/or different from the text structure of fiction being studied in class.

Creating Multimedia about Texts

After the students have read the opening chapters of the fiction work the class is studying and are through the exposition of that text and have a solid sense of the personalities of the characters, you could ask students to write a brief rationale, explaining why a particular literary character might be interested in some current event and what that character's response to those particular news stories might be. Following are some examples:

- Why would Jem in *To Kill a Mockingbird* be interested in a trial reported in the news media? What would he say about the verdict?
- Why would Mercutio or Benvolio in *Romeo and Juliet* be interested in curfew laws that require teenagers to be at home before 10 p.m.? What are some arguments for and against them?

- Why would Panchito from *The Circuit* or Esperanza from *Esperanza Rising* be interested in educational opportunities for undocumented immigrants? How would they advocate for more?

As you and the class continue studying the text, the students can be gathering information to flesh out persuasive speeches.

Or, in your class, students could read and reflect on a speech based on a topic they are studying in history, science, music, or math. Consider having students pattern the structure of a speech they like and present it as an example of a speech to inform, persuade, entertain, or commemorate. The introduction to their presentation should identify the rhetorical devices they are using and the text structures they will demonstrate.

Depending on your college setting and the access your students have to resources, you may need to provide in-class time for research as well as for practicing the speeches once they are written.

This kind of multi-genre and interdisciplinary assignment, looking at fiction and nonfiction concurrently in both print and electronic media, helps students make text-to-world connections. They can recognize that times change and people don't—a universal quality of good literature.

Since a portion of the assignment requires the students to justify their reasons for choosing the kinds of news articles and relating them to fictional characters, this assignment requires your student readers to consider how their fiction authors reveal the personalities and motivations of characters in the novels. Finally, including in your lesson a speech based on real news articles in the same instructional unit as the study of a novel gives students a chance to distinguish the different text structures used in fiction and nonfiction, a critical thinking skill most general-education course designers expect college students to develop.

CONCLUSION

Teaching students to read essays and view the speeches and media critically helps them become effective and sophisticated readers, viewers, listeners, and thoughtful creators in various formats. Students become more sensitive to the impact color, size, and design have on their intended audience when given the opportunity to create and present to their classmates on topics that matter to them.

Chapter Seven

Taking "TIME" to Teach Poetry

Words stir me
When I hear them
When I read them
When I write them
When I speak them

Words urge me
To keep listening
To keep reading
To keep writing
To keep speaking.

Let me hear you,
so I can know you.
Let me speak,
so you can know me.

Prodigiously stirring words
help me know you.
And viscerally urging words
help me know me.

–Anna J. Small Roseboro[1]

For some reason, students are apprehensive about studying poetry. And many college instructors also share a similar apprehension about teaching it, so, if you fall into this camp, you're in good company. Perhaps because of past experiences, students believe there is a key or secret code to understanding this genre, and only educators have the key to decipher that code. Experienced readers know that is not the case; it is a matter of understanding the genre and approaching poetry in a different way—paying special attention to poets' careful selection and arrangement of words.

The sample lessons in this chapter are designed to help you develop classroom experiences to systematically review and revive—and maybe overcome—what students may have learned previously. You will find strategies that can help students approach, read, understand, analyze, and write about classical, contemporary, structured, and free-verse poetry. Your blend of students, from different areas of town, the country, or the world, will be expected to read closely as they further refine critical skills of reading, writing, speaking, listening, and viewing while using technology for learning, publishing, and showing what they know. Most importantly, do what you can to help students *enjoy* reading, writing, and talking about poetry and also to create their own.

PREPARING TO TEACH POETRY

Scrounge up as many books of poetry as you can lug to class during this unit. Surf the web and familiarize yourself with diverse poems that you see other college teachers are using. Create virtual documents and slides with hot links you can share with your students. This search for poems will enhance your confidence in your readiness to teach this unusual genre that can be written as fiction or nonfiction. To make this a really rich experience for your

What should students know about poetry to succeed in college and in life?
https://www.istockphoto.com/photo/unsure-student-holding-pen-during-class-gm660503384-120432319

students, having a ready trove of poems for them to mine during their study of poetry is vital.

Do what you can so you and your learners have ready access to the trove you gathered. Assemble a list of websites to post as a hyperlinked list on your webpage so students can reference that list on homework assignments. One of the best is NCTE.org, with an entire collection of poetry-themed journals posted on that site.[2] See the companion website at www.teachingenglishlanguagearts.com for a list of collections and links to inspect and select as resources you can make available for students to peruse and use. Poetry Foundation provides another great site for poetry.

Even if you are in a high-tech setting, it's good to have multiple print books on hand. There's just something about touching a book and fingering the pages that deepens appreciation for the written word.

Using a Poem to Introduce Poetry Analysis

Begin with a poem to explain the process. Consider the poem "Unfolding Bud" by Naoshi Koriyama.[3] Post or project the poem where students can see it when they arrive on the first day of your direct instruction on poetry reading. This short poem provides a useful metaphor for the experience students have when they read and seems to allay some of their anxiety about understanding this genre of literature. You may also hand out copies, but refrain from reading the poem aloud. Instead, without saying anything, let students look at it for a couple of minutes. Sometimes silence gives space for student learning.

Now use a multiple-readings format; it works like this. Ask students to read the poem silently, paying attention to the punctuation and marking words or phrases that catch their attention. Next, read the poem aloud yourself. Then do one or both versions of "jump-in" oral reading. In version one, invite students to read a line at a time. Let them volunteer and begin reading on their own. At the end of the line, that student stops reading, and without raising a hand another student reads to the end of the succeeding line until the end of the poem.

Initially, there may be a giggle or even a gasp when more than one of them begins reading aloud at the same time. Assure them that it's fine. Just have them start over and encourage those who jump in at the same time to listen to each other and read together as one voice. It usually takes three or four false starts before they get the idea and are comfortable reading aloud this way. Others continue jumping in to read until the end of the poem.

In version two of "jump-in" reading, the first student reads and stops at the first mark of punctuation (comma, semicolon, period, question mark, etc.). Another person, without raising a hand, continues reading until the next punctuation mark. Again, if more than one student begins reading at the same time, have them begin again, listening to one another and reading as one voice.

Relax and allow the pauses between readers to be moments of resonation and reflection. False starts encourage students to pay attention to the words, lines, and punctuation and, thus, expand their understanding of the poem. The different single voices and blend of multiple voices resonate meaning and message.

This first lesson is a good time to talk about the value of multiple readings and why they often are necessary for understanding this condensed form of literature. The "Unfolding Bud" poem is a great conversation starter for this topic because Koriyama compares reading a poem to watching a water lily bud unfold. It takes time but is worth the wait.

Finding Messages Rather than Meanings

When teaching poetry, resist the temptation to ask students what the poem "means." This phrase incorrectly suggests there is only one meaning for a poem. The phrase "what it says" encourages students to look at the individual words and respond with a literal meaning, which can be the first step to analyzing poetry. But the specific choice and order of words all work to create images, the currency of poetry. Its goal is to create a sensory experience.

It is imperative to have students acknowledge and voice their initial response to the poem before moving on. What does the poem make them feel or connect with? Grounding students in their first response empowers them, and they begin to see themselves as capable readers of poetry. It is *their* reading. They build from there. The subsequent steps include determining whether the poem is saying something about a bigger issue or idea and whether the poem is speaking metaphorically. This approach gives students an opportunity to consider what they are learning in other classes about other times and other cultures.

Some poets may not have begun writing their poems about big universal issues; they may have written simply to recreate a very personal incident, observation, or experience. Yet, when read by others, their poem speaks to readers about issues quite different from the literal ideas that the poets originally intended to address. Often these bigger ideas do not emerge or manifest themselves on first or second readings. "Unfolding Bud" closes with the lines "over and over again," which suggests that poetry is somewhat different from other genres, and our understanding of it, more often than not, benefits from multiple readings.

Reading Poems in Alternative Ways

If you would rather not use "jump-in" reading to introduce the unit, slowly read the poem aloud yourself or share a recording of someone reading it, allowing time for the words to make their impact. Many well-done readings are available online. Again, check the Poetry Outloud website. Then ask a student to read the poem according to the punctuation, rather than just stopping at the end of each line. This second reading helps classmates focus on the fact that poems sometimes include punctuation, and that the punctuation serves the same function in poetry as in prose.

Punctuation clarifies the meaning of words organized in a particular order. It still is beneficial to have a third student read the poem aloud, who by this time may have an idea of what the poet may be trying to express. This third reader may choose to emphasize different words or read at a different pace, offering a third level of understanding. Either approach—"jump-in" reading or multiple readings—demonstrates the value of repetition in allowing a poem time to reveal itself to readers and listeners.

Defining Poetry: A Foundation for Discussion

Now, on the first day of the unit, is a prime time to explore a definition of poetry, this distinctive genre of literature that sometimes baffles new readers and at other times thrills them with its versatility. Use the definition in your anthology or the one that follows.

> Poetry is literature designed to *convey* a vivid and imaginative sense of experience, especially by the use of *condensed* language *chosen* for its sound and *suggestive* power as well as for its meaning and by the use of such literary devices as *structured* meter, *natural cadences*, rhyme and metaphor.[4]

Read the definition aloud a couple of times, letting your voice emphasize the italicized words. Then dictate it slowly so students can write the definition in their journals. Yes, allot time for the students actually to key in the words themselves. The heuristic of writing comes into play in that what they write or key in, they are more likely to recall later. Afterward, project the definition so they can verify their writing.

Why this laborious start? Hearing, listening, writing, and viewing are ways to reinforce the concept. This definition will form the basis of subsequent reflections on the form and function of poetry studied throughout the unit. Having a definition of a specific genre of writing aids close reading and a deeper understanding of the genre as well as how to make sense of the genre as students experiment with writing it.

Take a few moments more and ask students what they think the italicized words mean in the context of poetry. If no one offers suggestions, direct them to locate the words in a print or digital dictionary and to share the definitions with the class. If the students have been away from formal education for multiple years, this small step will save time later. With a firm foundation, they'll spring ahead, perhaps in a sprint.

Now return to the poem "Unfolding Bud" or a poem you've chosen and again ask the class what they imagine either poem is saying to them about reading poetry. What elements of the definition have Koriyama and your chosen poet used in their poems?

To solidify understanding, end the lesson by having students read aloud in unison the definition of poetry they have written in their notes, and then, like a Greek chorus, read one of the opening poems. The left side of the class can read stanza one; the right side, stanza two; and, in unison, the whole class can read stanza three. If they are taking a break, ask them to return with links to lyrics of their favorite song. Spend a little time linking song lyrics to poems, and students will see they are more familiar with this genre than they had supposed.

Swimming around in Poems

For homework, you can assign students to peruse their textbook or the websites you will have gathered and shared on your learning platform. Ask the students to flip through the book or scroll through those posted online to read a number of self-selected poems and then list four or five of them (titles and poets) in their notebooks. If such an out-of-class assignment is not a realistic expectation for the students you have, during the next class meeting, provide in-class time for them to look through their anthology or the poetry books you have collected for their use in the classroom.

Ask each student to select and copy into his or her own notebook the complete text of one or two poems from their list that attract their attention. They will likely choose short poems, and that's OK. For those using computers, have them key in the poem rather than simply copying and pasting. The physical act of handwriting or keying in the poem slows them down a bit so they can pay attention to (1) individual words, (2) line structure, and (3) pattern in poetry, three distinguishing features of this genre of literature.

Your students now have a self-selected poem to refer to and share with the class later during the unit. The value of this assignment is that it gives them an opportunity to read a variety of poems for which they are not required to do anything more than choose one they like. And the bonus? They are likely to read twice as many poems this way than if you were to assign a specific one to read for class. During the next class meeting, simply record in the grade book whether or not each student has a poem. The goal here is to get them to read poetry and become more at ease with this literary form.

Preparing to Speak Inspires Confident Verbal Articulating

Another way to utilize class time to practice skills prior to speaking and writing is to devote time for students to talk together in structured conversation. You might choose to use the template of Poetry Discussion Groups Job Descriptions based on the work of Kimberly Athans in "Poetry is a Vibe! Engaging Students with Poetry" (2023) and in other articles she has published in various teaching journals, based on her years of teaching students in high-school, community-college, and university settings in California and Texas.[5]

You may recognize the roles of discussion group participants as versions of the "Literature Circles" linked to the pedagogy of Harvey Daniels in the 1990s. The key is that individual students address, one at a time, the variety of perspectives we ask students to consider when they prepare to write about their experiences and reflections as they read and prepare to write academic essays or present oral or multimodal presentations. Athans describes these roles for discussing poetry:

BIOGRAPHER: What facets of the poet's background influenced their writing? Situate the poem in a social/historical context. Provide a lens. . . .

LINE LEADERS: Select three powerful or impressive lines from the poem and comment on why they appeal to you. Point out words and/or allusions that you notice help convey a message from the poet.

POET LAUREATE: Point out at least three different poetic devices the poet has utilized to convey the message, create tone, evoke a mood, or the way you respond to the poem. Would the same colors show the poet's tone and your mood? Why? Why not?

ILLUSTRATOR: Poetry is imagery. Use your personal artistic skills or find online resources to create a collage of images depicting the figurative language the poet has employed.

LITERARY CRITIC: Locate an article of criticism of the specific poem that you may find on websites (poets.org) and highlight key points and ideas. Share your discoveries. Do you agree or disagree? Why? If a student is unable to locate critiques of the specific poem, direct the student to search for and share a critique of the poet's work in general. It may appear on the rear of a book of poetry by this poet.

Using Popular Song Lyrics to Familiarize Students with Poetry

Encourage students to bring in song lyrics that are appropriate for sharing in class. Having them bring in song lyrics and poems of their choice also is a way for you to become more familiar with what your current students listen to and find interesting. They also will feel as though they are a part of the learning process because they are helping shape the lessons. Depending on the students you teach, you may wish to collect and read the lyrics first, then use them for a lesson later in the unit. Be alert to "trigger topics" that may cause hard feelings or strong reactions. There is no need to avoid such topics; just show students how to listen to alternative views with the same empathy they want when they express themselves.

T.I.M.E.: A STRATEGY FOR POETRY ANALYSIS

Poetry "TIME" has been around for decades as a strategy for introducing poetry analysis and has been passed along from teacher to teacher across the nation. You, too, may have been taught this way and find this clever acronym to be just what you need to organize your instruction and enhance student learning. If you choose to use it, you are likely to have former students return to express their appreciation for having a mnemonic that has served them well on standardized and placement tests as well as on final exams in other courses. In relation to poetry, the letters T.I.M.E. stand for (1) title, thought, and theme; (2) imagery; (3) music; and (4) emotion, expressed by the author and experienced by the reader or listener.

Knowing this acronym gives students a place to start and can help them unlock meaning in poetry. As they have learned in their readings of the Koriyama poem and others' selections, poems are written in a condensed language and often require multiple readings. TIME really is a pun and refers not only to the fact that it often takes more time to read and write poetry but also refers to elements of a poem that, when considered independently, can lead to a deeper understanding of the poem in its entirety. Taking TIME for poetry will help students recognize subtleties of the genre that the authors may have conscientiously or unconsciously woven together in the creation of their poem.

Letter "T" Stands for Title, Thought, Theme

Begin with T, for the title of a poem. If a poet has chosen a title, it often serves as an indication of what the poem is about and may suggest the emotion or opinion the poet has about the experience related in the poem. The title may serve as a peephole into the interior of the poem, which the reader will explore once inside. The T also could stand for the thought or theme of the poem. This is a flexible acronym, and you can decide the best word(s) to use with the students you have. You may use one, two, or three of these T words. All are related to the study of this genre.

Consider poems published by Poetry Without Borders, mentioned in the Harvard General Education program, and the "Practice of Poetry" at the Appalachian State University, and course-content information offered by the University of Illinois: Urbana campus. Another great source for poetry and teaching resources is the Poetry Foundation website (poetryfoundation.org).

Next, draw the students' attention to concepts about the speaker and audience. Published poetry is meant to be understood. You may choose to clarify this idea and specify "published poetry" because many people write poetry just for themselves and may not care whether anyone else even reads it, let alone understands it. Generally, though, a poet is someone saying something to someone. That first someone is "the speaker," who may or may not be the poet. Be alert, as well, to the fact that contemporary poets may not use pronouns in the same way used in the previous century. That is yet another reason for considering the context in which a piece of writing has been written.

For example, you may have a poet, an elderly woman who writes a poem in the persona of an adolescent boy. In this particular situation, the poet is a woman, and the speaker in the poem is a boy. Looking at the kind of pronouns used, the vocabulary and images can help the reader imagine the audience. One visual way that helps students think of poetry as a piece of writing with a message is to use a graphic design with three spaces: one large rectangle in the middle of the page, one small circle on the left, and one or more circles on the right of the large rectangle.

After they make this full-page chart in the poetry section of their journals, ask your students to draw a picture of a possible speaker in the small circle on the left and to draw, in the circle(s) on the right, a possible audience: one person, a special person, or a group of people. Then, in the rectangle in the center, have students write a one-sentence summary of what the poem could be saying and quote a couple lines from the poem to support their opinion.

Demonstrate this task by returning to the poem you used to introduce the unit or use the poem, "Words, Words, Words," that introduces this chapter. To further demonstrate, repeat the exercise using the poem "Unfolding Bud" by Koriyama. Draw the graphic organizer on the board and then ask students, "Who could be the speaker?" and "Who could be the audience?"

For the Koriyama poem, typical answers include a parent talking to a student who is having difficulty with homework, trying to persuade the young person to hang in there and not give up just because the poem is difficult to understand after one or two readings. Some may share that they think it is a teacher speaking to an individual student or the class as a whole.

To reinforce the concepts of speaker and audience, distribute a copy of Emily Dickinson's poem, "I'm Nobody."[6] Ask the students to read it and think of as many different speaker and audience sets as they can. Ask them to imagine this poem was to be spoken by a character in a play or movie. What could be the setting? Who could be the speaker? Who is the audience? The only limitation is that the sets must be supported by the words of the poem. Your students may come up with combinations or settings, such as the following:

- A student new to high school talking to another student in the cafeteria
- A nontraditional student returning to college and attending her very first class
- A new graduate student assistant at the first department meeting
- A hip-hop artist waiting to perform on a TV program
- A parent talking to another parent during the college orientation event
- A person attending a neighborhood luncheon for the first time

If you are in the mood, act a little silly, ham it up, and reread the poem in the voices and personae of the pairs the students suggest. Invite students to do a couple of the combos. Great fun! This activity makes the point, too, of a poem having multiple possibilities but common meanings.

Letter "I" Stands for the Imagery in Poetry

Poets use words to help create pictures, emotions, ideas, or memories of incidents in the minds of readers and listeners, using sensory or figurative images or a combination of the two. Sensory imagery, you recall, appeals to one or more of the five senses: sight, hearing, taste, touch, and smell. It is through our senses that we experience the world, and many poets appeal to them as they recreate their own experiences in poetic form.

Rather than presenting this portion of the lesson as a lecture, simply draw or project the image of an eye, an ear, a mouth, a hand, and a nose on the board. Then, ask the students to label the drawings and give examples of words or phrases that appeal to the senses. Prepare for the lesson by looking at a variety of poems, compiling sample lines from poems that illustrate appeals to the various senses. Better yet, invite students to offer lines they recall from familiar song lyrics, but be prepared with your examples just to prime the pump . . . to get them thinking.

This would be a good time to ask students to look back at the poems they selected and copied into their journals at the beginning of the unit. Set your timer for five minutes and have them look at the poem and mark images. Then, reset the timer for ten minutes, have students pull their desks together or turn to a table partner, and then share, pointing out examples of sensory images from their chosen poems.

Working with poems they have chosen validates the assignment to choose and copy poems into their notebooks. Invite volunteers to read aloud to the class any lines that illustrate the sensory images they find. Variety spices the lessons and increases interest.

Next, direct their attention to figurative imagery. Many of your students will have learned about similes and metaphors in precollegiate coursework and will be able to define them for the class. Some know "personification"; fewer know "hyperbole" and "symbol" and "allusion." Be prepared to introduce these devices and give students definitions and examples. If you notice that most of your students are nodding their heads as you read through the list of poetic devices, go ahead and add some of the less widely used but equally effective strategies poets employ to relay their messages. Consider adding allegory, anaphora, antistrophe, and epistrophe.

Occasionally a poet uses a *symbol*—something concrete that stands for something else: an abstract concept, another thing, an idea, or an event. For example, a "flag" is a cloth on a stick. But a certain configuration of colors and shapes, such as stars on a blue rectangular field in the upper left corner of a red-and-white-striped cloth, suggests the American flag, which stands for the nation, freedom, democracy, and patriotism.

Symbols can be a great opening to talk about cultural contexts, too. For example, a snake or serpent symbolizes different ideas depending on the culture, the religion, or the nation. Red in some cultures is a sad color, representing blood or anger; in other cultures, it is a happy color, representing marriage or royalty. The owl in one culture is a sign of wisdom. In another, this same bird is an omen of death.

An *allusion* is a reference to another body of literature, a movie, or an incident the writer believes the readers know. Allusions can help the writer create an image with just a few words because the writer believes that, by referencing them in the poem, the allusion automatically triggers memories, ideas, or emotions.

In Western literature, allusions frequently are made to *The Holy Bible* with its Hebrew and Christian scriptures; Roman and Greek mythology; Shakespeare's writings; and fairy tales. Sometimes a reference may be made to classic movies like *Gone with the Wind*, *The Wizard of Oz*, *Star Trek*, or the more recent *Black Panther* movie. Or the reference could be to a historical incident like the Civil War or the Gold Rush. If your students represent a range of cultures and national origins, select samples from the literature and historical events that are more familiar to them. Consider stories, myths, and sacred texts they may know from literature and life in Central America, South America, Asia, India, Africa, and Australia.

You could spend the remainder of the class time looking at examples of poems that have strong imagery. Project copies of two poems already discussed as a class. Then ask students to find examples of multiple kinds of imagery to share and compare with a partner and encourage them to copy favorite lines into their journals. Remember, in order to find their own examples, students will read much more poetry than if you provided all the samples yourself. Equally important is the fact that, in each year you teach the unit, you continue to learn and discover the kinds of poems that interest students in each different class.

Patterning Poetry—Teacher and Student Responses

An assignment that always evokes positive responses and results in some pretty good poetry is one on patterning poems. In this activity, also referred to as "mimic poems," students are asked to imitate or emulate the form and language of another poem. Think of it as fanfiction for poetry.

Ask students to select one or two of the poems that they particularly like either from their anthology or from the list you have compiled and shared on your learning platform. Next, ask them to think of a memorable experience of their own. The selected poem will often inspire the student's memory. Finally, invite your learners to pattern the structure and imagery of one of their chosen poems to recreate the experience of their incident. Of course, if you are writing poems along with them (and you should), you experience how it feels to write on demand as you are asking them to do. Then you, too, have something newly written to read during sharing time.

For example, you could ask your students to write a lyric poem like Robert Frost's "Acquainted with the Night," then share with your learners a poem (shown below) that Anna wrote when her students were doing this patterning activity. Go ahead, ask them to evaluate the poem to discover how many of Frost's strategies her poem reflects. She hopes they give her at least a "B" for effort.

> I have been one acquainted with that song
> I've sung the song in tune and out of tune
> I have held that high note oh so long
>
> I have sung that song—clear like a loon
> I have kept within the music's beat
> Swooped down low, yet staying right in tune.
> I've sung that song and let my voice just soar

While deep within my soul, the words brought tears
That slipped right down my cheeks, my heart just tore.

That song reminding me of trials sore
Experienced by people who did so long
For freedom, justice, rights and so much more.

The freedoms they had waited for too long
I have been one acquainted with that song.

by Anna J. Small Roseboro

Consider other poems for patterning: "So Much Depends" or "This is Just to Say," by William Carlos Williams; "Stopping By the Woods on a Snowy Evening" by Robert Frost; "Still I Rise" by Maya Angelou; "in just Spring" by e e cummings.

As you might expect, there are also poem-generator sites where you can plug in topics, images, forms, and other elements, and the generator will produce a poem. After having students attempt emulating a poem on their own, it might be fun to share some of the generator sites and then have students critique the results. For example, the NCTE ReadWriteThink website offers lessons using online tools and apps for teaching poetry.

Letter "M" Stands for Music

According to the definition of poetry used earlier, poets choose words "for their sound and suggestive power." Now let's look at three aspects of song lyrics and poetry: (1) rhythm, (2) rhyme, and (3) the sound of words. Some poets arrange their words to create a pattern of beats or *rhythm*. Your students may recall learning the "ITADS," an acronym for five common poetic rhythm patterns: iambic, trochaic, anapestic, dactylic, and spondee. These terms identify the patterns of stressed and unstressed syllables, information students surely are expected to know by the time they get into college-level coursework.

During this lesson on the music or sound elements of poetry, mention to the students that ITADS patterns are called the "feet" of poetry. There is only one stressed syllable in each foot. Explain that a poem's rhythm, or the "meter," is named for the number of feet or beats per line and the kind of foot that is in each line.

For example, a line of poetry with four feet or four beats is tetrameter ("tetra," Greek for four). If the feet are iambic—one unstressed syllable followed by a stressed one—the line is identified as iambic tetrameter. Have fun by asking students to identify the rhythm patterns of their own names. Anna is trochaic. Jamar is iambic. Small is spondee. Roseboro is dactylic. What are the patterns of your name?

Moving to the Rhythm of Poetry

Because many students are kinesthetic learners and can remember what they feel physically, you should demonstrate the rhythms of poetry that way, too. Read a poem with a strong beat while students are standing up and marching in place. How about inviting them to clap their hands, tap one foot, or snap their fingers to the beat?

To use that abundance of energy, have the students march around the room when you read William Wordsworth's poem "Daffodils": "I wander'd lonely as a cloud." Rather than wandering quietly, stomp loudly. Use your arms to sway broadly from side to side to show the rhythm of the waves in John Masefield's "Sea Fever": "I *must* go down to the seas again, to the *lonely* sea and the sky." Of course, your learners understand right away the rhythm of song lyrics, but you could save this until later. For now, acknowledge that "Just as some poetry has a specific rhythm pattern, so do the lyrics or words of some songs you know." If you have time, invite a couple of students to locate on their tablet or phone the lyrics of a song with a strong beat. Read the lyrics rather than listening to the music. Play a recording of a current popular rap song. Point made! Yes, this kind of physical activity is an efficient way to revive energy in a class of adults who may be exhausted from a busy day or bored with what has been going on in class so far.

Listening for Patterns of Sounds

A second way to look at the sounds of poetry is to consider the *rhyme*, which occurs when words with similar sounds are used in an observable pattern. The rhyme may occur at the end of a line or within a line.

Students can discover the pattern of rhyme by using letters of the alphabet to indicate repeated sounds. For example, begin writing with the letter "a" at the end of the first line of poetry. If the second line ends with the same sound, write "a" again. If it ends with a different sound, change to "b." Continue throughout the poem to determine if there is a pattern and what the pattern is.

The narrative poem "The Cremation of Sam McGee," by Robert W. Service, makes particularly interesting reading when you are teaching internal and end rhyme. The macabre story is intriguing, too. Check out the online versions in which Service and Johnny Cash each have recorded their renditions of this narrative poem. Your students may enjoy the photos, too.

Be alert, as well, to the fact that students for whom English is a language they don't speak very much may not readily notice rhyme in English poetry just by reading it. What they see on the page may not "translate" into words that sound alike. Consider homophones like "ate and eight"; "break and brake"; "hire and higher"; and "sore, sour, and sewer."

Point out that free- and blank-verse poetry have no systematic rhyme pattern. You probably plan to discuss this kind of poetry later in your unit, but go ahead and mention it now, particularly if students bring in examples of free-verse poetry or notice it in their class anthology. This is why it is good to begin the unit with the definition of poetry that mentions structured meter or natural cadences. Your discussion of the music of poetry gives space to talk about blank- and free-verse poetry without having to provide another definition or having to backpedal when they point out that some poetry is unstructured in terms of rhythm and rhyme.

All of these poetic elements work together and create a synergy allowing the reader to "experience" the poem. Remember that the goal of poetry is to create an aesthetic response. It's about the overall experience, not just figuring out some meaning.

Seeing Song Lyrics as Poetry

Now is a perfect time to ask selected students to read aloud lyrics of their favorite songs. Most have a steady beat and many rhyme, making the connection between poetry in music and poetry in books easier to comprehend. Consider the work of Smokey Robinson, Bruce Springsteen, Jule, Taylor Swift, and Bob Dylan. Be prepared for students to show more interest in what they bring to the class.

Show your enthusiasm as you look at and listen to what students bring. They might share rock, rap, folk, country, or Broadway music. Regardless, they are providing you a window into their worlds and what you learn reveals what they know and indicates what you may need to teach or reteach as you continue planning learning experiences for your poetry unit. Combine the familiar with the new by encouraging your students to use the vocabulary of poetry as they talk about song lyrics they choose themselves.

If you have the nerve, you can "prove" the link between poetry and music by singing the "I'm Nobody" poem to the tune of either "Yellow Rose of Texas" or "America, the Beautiful"! Even if you are a very good singer, the students probably are going to laugh at you, but they also will remember the lesson. Is that not the goal of teaching? Or, do a quick online search. You'll be able to find examples of well-known poems that have been recorded as songs.

Sensory Image of Sounds

A third way to talk about the music or sound of poetry is to point out *ono-matopoeia*, words that are spelled to imitate the sound they describe. Some students will love making peculiar, sometimes shocking, and vulgar noises. One way to exploit that particular pleasure is to have the students write poems that capture the sounds of everyday experiences. One of Anna's students, Warren, wrote "The Kitchen" about the sounds at home. Like Shakespeare, Warren enjoys making up words, too.

> With a cling clang
> Not a bang or dang
> a swish and a wish
> all the dishes are in the sink
> screech creach
> open
> close
> scuffles ruffles
> a sea of bubbles and water
> a crounging rounging
> with a turn of the knob
> all the dishes are clean
> then click click click
> whoosh.
> Are you hungry for lunch yet?

Another way to address sound as you discuss the music of poetry is to consider repetition of vowels (*assonance*) or consonants (*alliteration* or *consonance*). Most students recognize tongue twisters as examples of alliteration. Keep these terms in mind when you are teaching persuasive writing and speech making. Nonfiction writers often use the sound of words to create memorable sound bites of their arguments and calls to action.

Letter "E" Stands for Emotions

The emotion expressed by the poet and the emotion experienced by the reader may very well be different. How do students discover these emotions? By paying attention to the kinds of images (comparisons to positive or negative things) and the music, rhyme, rhythm, and sounds of words the poet uses to convey the experience of the poem.

The students may find examples of emotions expressed, such as pride, love, grief or distress, fear, joy, jealousy, or shame or embarrassment. They may experience similar feelings as they read or hear the poems, but the emotion expressed and experienced often is not the same! There will also be a broad range of responses among those in class. Remind them that we filter everything we read through our own prior experience. What triggers a strong reaction from one reader may not have that same effect on another because he or she hasn't had identical experiences. Have students try their new analyzing skills by reading and talking about "The Boy in the Window" by Richard Wilbur.

Remind your students that the "tone" of a poem refers to the author's attitude or feeling about the topic or experience related in the poem. On the other hand, "mood" refers to the way the poem makes the reader feel when they read or hear the poem. To help make the link more personal, you can draw their attention to the M in mood and say, "Mood means the way the poem makes ME, the reader, feel." That usually is sufficient instruction at this time.

As you teach these poetry terms, continue to encourage your learners to use them regularly when talking and writing about poetry. Such use raises the level of their conversation, expands their working vocabulary, and helps to build their confidence. It makes them feel oh, so sophisticated!

Emotional Power of Sounds

Students are intrigued to learn that the sound of words suggests certain emotions, too. For example, a poet who wishes to convey the emotion or sense of experience in a calm, peaceful way is likely to select soft-sounding consonants, like *l*, *m*, *n*, and *s*. If the memory is unpleasant or bitter, the poet is likely to pick hard consonants that must be forced through the lips and teeth to be formed, like *p*, *t*, and *f*, or guttural sounds, like *k*, *g*, and *j*. A graphic way to illustrate this can be by pointing out that most obscene words in English include these harsh, guttural, and dental sounds.

Of course, you need not say them aloud or write them down. Students know the words if you refer to "the F word" or "the S word." They smile and smirk, and your point is made. If many of your students speak other languages, and if you can maintain control of the class, you may ask them if profane words in their language follow this pattern of harsh sounds. Again, let them think, but not speak, the words. The point is made.

SPENDING "TIME" READING POEMS INDEPENDENTLY

One way for students to practice reading on their own without feeling undue pressure is to ask them to continue bringing in poems and to point out the ways their self-selected poems reflect the various elements already studied.

This subtly entices them to read more widely. They are likely to return to the books skimmed before and come across poems that speak to them differently this time.

Giving this assignment again also reveals to you how students' choice of poetry is being modified by the series of lessons you are teaching. Invite them to post their choices on your class website, remembering to include the title, author, and source on a page on the class website, entitled "Poems We Like." Consider the "student starter" lesson plan for which students sign up to read aloud their chosen poems at the start of class. It takes only a minute or two, and, after the first student shares, there will be others who also want to share and receive that acknowledgment.

As they seek out poems, encourage your students to interview family members to learn about their favorite poems. Call, email, or text the interviewee if necessary. It's surprising how amazed college students are to learn that their moms, dads, aunts, uncles, and even grandparents had to memorize and recite poetry as a regular part of their literature coursework! If they speak languages other than English at home, invite your learners to bring in poems by favorite poets in those languages and read them aloud to the class. This affirms their heritage and expands the cultural experience for you and their classmates as well.

You know to alert your students to the fact that poems address an array of topics in a variety of ways. Remind your eager learners to use their judgment about which poems would be appropriate to share in class. Fortunately, by this time in the course, you have established a classroom environment, and students know what constitutes sensitive reading and sensible selections. However, reminding them at this time is still a good idea.

Notice that your use of the term *message* or the term *theme* keeps the poem open for students to draw from it what the poem says to them. As soon as you suggest the "meaning," they begin guessing and hoping they come up with the "right" answer. With self-control, you can let the poems speak for themselves.

Transmigrating Flash Fiction

Transmigration in writing simply means moving the essence of one text into a different genre. In this case, we're suggesting transmigrating from a short story to poetry. Before you assign it, try it yourself. Read one or two works of *flash fiction* short stories in one thousand words or less, like those published by the *New York Times* or *The New Yorker* magazine, and written by writers of various cultures. Then, write a narrative poem, telling that same story in two hundred words or less. See online samples of *flash poetry* that may interest your students. There are specific sites dedicated to flash fiction, such as Flash

Fiction Online and Flash Fiction Magazine. Further along in this section is a first draft transmigrated poem written about a work from one of those sites; the short story is called "Paradise City," by Teresa Bassett.[7]

This can be an ungraded practice, so students will not be embarrassed and will be open to recommendations for improvement in the writing for the assignment described here.

Use whatever poetry style that works for you. Consider poems that have stanzas of five to seven lines and that include an exposition, a triggering action, rising action, a climax, falling action (a denouement), and a resolution for the work of flash fiction being transmigrated.

Students with whom you share the Teresa Bassett short story and Small Roseboro's poem will note the details that match and those that do not. Invite your students to evaluate how effectively the transmigrated poem fulfills this assignment. The following is Anna's attempt to transmigrate from Teresa Bassett's flash fiction short story, "Paradise City." Ask students to rate Anna's poem, "What Happened to Daddy?" using the guidelines you provide for their assignment.

Daddy is driving awfully fast
The music is jamming like a blast
We are spending a weekend with him at last
Sammy sits in the back with his fist
Dripping with snot from his nose.
He's just four years old. That's how it goes.

The glove compartment door swings open
I reach in for a tissue to clean . . . what?
Then gasp at what I have seen.
There's a gun in there and it's not a spare
It's the family gun, I know it. I've seen it before.

What's that I hear piercing my ear.
The sirens are coming closer and closer
And I notice Dad getting tense
So I slam the door shut and wait.

We near the river and Daddy turns down the trail
The trail to the edge of the water
He screeches to a stop and makes us get out
Then I hear the cops shout.

Dad picks up my brother and gives him a hug
The cops look at daddy like he's some kind of thug.
But he isn't. He just wanted to see us
Not go to jail. But now he must.

Reading flash fiction in class will take most students about ten minutes, then drafting the story in a short poem will take another ten to fifteen minutes, so using class time for such practice is practical. The students who read the same story can exchange poems and give feedback on what works and what needs a little more work to include the elements of the assignment in a more intriguing way.

Inviting students to summarize or transmigrate from one genre to another is just another way to have them pay attention to details. It does not matter if the poem rhymes or has a steady beat. The goal is to capture the essence of the experience in carefully chosen words.

Assigning the Poetry Project or Portfolio

As you plan to teach poetry in a more formal way, perhaps in a literature elective course, schedule time to assign an extensive poetry project that includes poems students select on a theme they choose and poems they write themselves on the same or related topic or theme.

An effective way to reinforce the interests raised and skills developed during a poetry unit is to have students assemble a poetry portfolio. The collection should include poems they have read and enjoyed as well as poems they have written themselves. A sample assignment comes next. Decide how much time you have to devote to this project and select activities that may be organized around one or more of the following topics:

- Poems by a single poet
- Poems written on a single theme (family, hobby, love, social justice, seasons, etc.)
- Poems employing common poetic devices
- Poems reflecting a specific culture or nationality

It is imperative to inform your learners at the beginning of the poetry unit if they are to create this poetry portfolio as part of their graded work. Knowing ahead of time, they can think about and collect poems throughout the weeks you spend on formal poetry study.

CONCLUSION

Few readers deny either that poets tend to write cryptically or that it takes more effort to discover what poets have to say to their listeners and readers. When you teach your students to tell the TIME of a poem, you give your new-to-college readers a golden key they can use for life. Using this key, they know to look systematically for different aspects of the poem on each rereading. They experience the delight of discovery and enthusiasm of empowerment when you give them TIME to study this genre of literature.

As when traveling in a new country, sampling new and different foods, students may even develop gustatory joy from sampling this genre of literary expression. Through the guided practice you offer, even squirmy college students slow down and pay attention to the words, form, sounds, and, eventually, messages in poetry. They may even astonish you when their careful reading leads to interpretations like those that published critics write about the poems!

By the end of your formal instruction in this course, your students will feel far more confident about studying this challenging literary genre. They may not have the ease of Huck Finn's friend Emmeline Grangerford and be able to "slap down a line . . . just scratch it out and slap down another one,"[8] but they now are able to read, write, and talk more confidently about poetry in their own way. Your empowered learners can respond to those "prodigiously stirring words" and feel comfortable putting pen to paper to capture the "viscerally urging words" that become poems of their own.

Chapter Eight

Reading to Write and Writing to Be Read

[R]eaders construct meaning by building multifaceted, interwoven representations of knowledge. The current text, prior texts, and the reading context can exert varying degrees of influence on this process, but it is the reader who must integrate information into meaning.[1]

–Christine Haas and Linda Flower

Before any lessons begin, it's important to lay the groundwork. Create curiosity by asking probing questions that inspire exploration of the various genres you are required to teach in your course. Prepare your students for the tasks of reading various genres and texts by defining terms, showing them patterns, and encouraging them to "notice and note" what they see in their reading, to use the terms in speaking, and to employ the strategies in writing for your course. If they use them, they won't lose them.

Many college classroom instructors and professors organize their courses thematically, based on topics important to them, as teachers. That's fine, but we must give students time to understand and appreciate those choices. Some teachers choose theses related to social and historical issues; others select writing by authors based on race, nationality, religion, or their interest in some natural phenomenon, like nature.

One summer, in a writing workshop on Sitka Island in Alaska, our leader chose essays and stories written about living and working in the natural environments found in the northwestern United States. Whatever theme you choose, keep the course goals in mind as you introduce, discuss, and assign reading and writing along the way.

COMPARING OTHER WAYS OF TEACHING

Keeping in mind that the students in your classes are likely to have been taught in different ways that may thwart their learning with you, consider inviting students to write about that. Nancy G. (Perkins) Kohl would invite her international students to compare and contrast one of the differences between their recent academic experiences in their home country and their recent academic experiences as students at the University of Massachusetts in Lowell. Generally, they write about the teachers' styles in classroom presentation of content material; student involvement during class time; homework expectations, deadlines, or amount; use of syllabi, types or usefulness of syllabi; and rules of decorum in the classroom, such as deadlines, cell phones, attendance, or being on time.

Inviting your students to reflect on and write informally about what they know already and consider what they are being asked to learn and do in your course can be an informative and insightful experience for both students and teachers. Gaining awareness of what students have done in the past helps instructors and professors understand current behaviors in class as they assign different genres and also understand students' responses to the reading and writing assignments.

SHOWING THEM HOW

Kia Jane Richmond, a professor and the director of English education at Northern Michigan University (NMU), teaches a course called "Good Books." The course, part of the NMU general-education program, is offered as an in-person course, as a virtual course, and as an asynchronous web-based course during the summer.

This "Good Books" class is an "exploration of a variety of books from the past and present for the general reader. Reading and discussing ideas from books with insights into human experiences are emphasized." She has selected the topic of *mental health* as an overarching theme to help students meet the "human expression" goal of demonstrating "analysis and evaluation of artistic, literary or rhetorical expression" in texts. Thus, whether they read fiction, nonfiction, or graphic novels, each book has a focus on mental illness in some way.

Among the various genres offered in the class are literary works like the following:

- *The Quiet Room*, by Lori Schiller with Amanda Bennett (1996), an adult, nonfiction work (a memoir)
- *The Absolutely True Diary of a Part-Time Indian*, by Sherman Alexie (2009), a young adult, fiction work
- *Hey, Kiddo*, by Jarrett J. Krosoczka (2018), a young adult, graphic nonfiction work (a memoir)
- *She's Come Undone*, by Wally Lamb (1998), an adult, fiction work

For one assignment, Richmond asks students to complete a rhetorical analysis of at least one book and invites students to explore questions such as the following:

1. What is the author's purpose for the text, and how do you know?
2. What can you determine about the author's ethos, credibility, or experiences, and how might those help you in understanding his or her positioning in relation to the subject matter?
3. What is the author's main argument, and how do you know? What kinds of evidence does the author provide to support claims (e.g., examples, reasoning, data, narratives)?
4. Who does the author lean on to give credence to arguments (e.g., experts in the field, scholars, laypersons, medical staff, etc.)?
5. How is the text organized, and what features does it include to help readers move through it (e.g., chapter titles, chapter summaries, headings, images/charts, bolded words, glossary)?
6. Who is the book written for, and how do you know?
7. What are some of the assumptions that the author makes about the audience?
8. How is the text similar to (or different from) other texts you have read (fiction, nonfiction, graphic novel, academic texts, biography, persuasive, etc.)?

Using rhetorical analysis can help nonfiction readers examine underlying assumptions, positionalities (referring to disclosure of the writer's own self-identifications and experiences and their influence on the writer), and values that are a part of a text's messages. By asking students to engage in this process, instructors facilitate learning, developing students' critical thinking and improving their ability to read nonfiction successfully. Of course, you also will be providing lessons, such as those described in chapter 6, for conducting research to answer some of the questions during rhetorical analysis that Richmond has passed along. What would be a theme you would employ to organize the texts you get to choose in the course you are hired to teach?

CHOOSING STUDENT-CENTRIC TEXTS

Presenting at the Journal of Language and Literacy Education (JoLLE) Virtual Conference at the University of Georgia (February 11, 2023), Ashley Brumbelow and Brittany Pope Thomason shared elements of their student-centric approach to social-justice education that includes ideas you may wish to consider. According to one of the slides they showed, this team's stated goal was "to create classroom communities that invite vulnerability and give students space to grow and become informed and curious individuals." These classroom teachers center their units around themes and topics, many of which are student-generated, that welcome exploration of diverse perspectives.

Among the texts they teach as a whole-class novel is *Just Mercy: A Story of Justice and Redemption*, by Bryan Stevenson.[2] This work of fiction invites students to read, reflect, discuss, and write their own critique of justice in the United States as it relates to issues of systemic racism, gender discrimination, and the impact of socioeconomic status.

One strategy Brumbelow and Thomason suggest using is the Socratic seminar during which students discuss rather than debate crucial questions posed in the text and presented by student discussion leaders. See myriad online sites that help prepare college classroom teachers to design lessons for this vigorous yet insightful way for their learners to come to an understanding about controversial issues.

Known classmates can now be the chosen audience.

https://www.istockphoto.com/photo/learning-concept-international-students-doing-group-study-in-library-gm1205264662-347130518

And these thoughtful educators find that using literature circles proves engaging when students have a choice of a variety of genres within teacher-approved texts. This pair of educators recommend the autobiography, *I Am Malala* (2013), by Malala Yousafzai; *The Other Wes Moore: One Name/Two Fates* (2010), by Wes Moore; *A Long Way Gone: Memoirs of a Boy Soldier* (2007), by Ishmael Beah; and a graphic novel, *March: Book One Paperback—Illustrated* (2013) by John Lewis, Andrew Aydin, and Nate Powell.

Various online sites describe a variety of roles students fill in literature circles. Roles range from discussion director, savvy summarizer, creative connector, and imaginative illustrator to character captain, travel tracker, word wizard, and literary luminary. Most educators select four or six roles per text, depending on the topics, students' interests, and time for prepping to fill the roles.

As students experience a variety of texts focusing on mining and exploring how authors write different genres so readers keep reading, assign short in-class modeling activities where students demonstrate their understanding of these elements of the genre and approaches to relating. The students then can model what they read in their own writing-to-be-read. Getting comments from classmates is next.

USING AVATARS TO INFUSE FEEDBACK

Sometimes assuming a novel role helps students focus in novel ways to provide courteous and constructive feedback to the second or third drafts of their classmates' writing. Jessica Hudson, a visiting professor at Principia College, Elsah, Illinois, teaches general-education writing strategies courses. She has a really clever way of getting her students thinking about literary rhetorical devices.

She has them assume personae based on the Nickelodeon television show, *Avatar: The Last Airbender*. Many students have seen or at least heard of *Avatar*, which helps motivate them to participate in this fun revision activity. In this case, students choose or are assigned an AVATAR element of earth, water, fire, or air, to use as a lens through which to read and respond to classmates' essay drafts. As students read, they are to focus specifically on their chosen element, taking notes as they read in order to comment using their assigned FONT COLOR once they complete reading that classmates' draft. Each reviewer is to write two examples of where their assigned element is working well and two recommendations for revising this particular element within the writing—fiction or nonfiction.

1. RIVER TO OCEAN: As a river flows for miles and miles and finally arrives at the ocean, so writing flows from introduction to conclusion, paragraph by paragraph. The WATER REVISER studies this flow and, using BLUE font, comments on the text's trajectory.
2. The core idea of a piece of writing provides the foundation for structure, content, and tone. The EARTH REVISER studies this foundation and notes the cracks that may be weakening the structure as a whole and, using GREEN font, comments on what is strong and what may be done to shore up the writing.
3. BURN BRIGHT: Every draft has sections that resonate strongly and sections that are, essentially, deadwood. The FIRE REVISER studies the writer's diction (word choice) and comments in RED font on where and how this piece could burn even more brightly.
4. THE FLOW: Effective writing flows smoothly and logically from idea to idea, paragraph to paragraph, enabling readers to follow it. The AIR REVISER studies these transitions and comments in YELLOW font on the movement of ideas within and between paragraphs.

By the end of the class time set for this practice, the students will have colorfully written comments from their peers' writing. They'll have a better sense of the value of the FLOW from the introduction to the conclusion

Circulate, observe, and assist as needed.

from the WATER AVATAR and ideas of the strength of the CORE from the EARTH AVATAR, who will have focused on the main ideas. Student writers will feel empowered to address issues relating to diction and tone by reading the well-worded comments from the FIRE AVATAR and will be reminded of the effectiveness of TRANSITIONS from what the AIR AVATAR will have noted and mentioned in comments.

Being a giver and a receiver of comments benefits your learners in multiple ways. They will have read in four roles and written in response to their class-mates' comments from four different perspectives and received colorfully explicit comments on which to reflect as they revise the text of the writing you will have assigned them to compose.

There can be much flexibility in this assignment. See the chart about sched-uling speeches in chapter 6. You may adapt that rotation as a way to lay out this avatar reviser plan. This peer feedback structure offers an approach to laying out which student reads what and in what role. Check out the video Jessica Hudson shared at a recent National Council of Teachers of English Annual Convention. The link is on the PLANNING WITH PURPOSE website.

CONCLUSION

Continue to design framed lessons that show students ways to read more attentively to what works. Allot time for process writing where students model what they read, draft writing, and create a variety of papers, products, and presentations to show their learning in oral and multimedia performances. Building in time for giving and receiving feedback from peers, revising and sharing their learning in person and online, is a teaching strategy that can significantly reduce at-home grading for you.

As you incorporate intentional teaching of reading different genres and texts into your general-education courses, you will empower your students to achieve a wider variety of skills needed for success in later courses and on into life in general. Keep in mind that the teacher is not just a pitcher pouring information into receptacles, but a co-learner who guides students along the journey of learning. Educators who are professionally successful and person-ally satisfied as classroom teachers maximize the opportunity to learn with their diverse student bodies.

Each time you design flexible lessons permeated with rich experiences for exploring fiction and nonfiction in print and electronic media, you move your students further along the road to success. Each time you risk writing with them, when you assign writing in a range of genres and rhetorical styles for a variety of authentic purposes and audiences, you demonstrate the importance of vulnerability in a learning community and honesty in writing.

Notes

INTRODUCTION

1. Phil Collins, "Son of Man," Sound Track Lyrics, https://www.stlyrics.com/lyrics/tarzan/sonofman.htm.

CHAPTER ONE

1. Steven Mintz, "How to Improve College Teaching in 2023," *Higher Ed Gamma* (blog), Inside Higher Ed, 9 January 2023, https://www.insidehighered.com/blogs/higher-ed-gamma/how-improve-college-teaching-2023.

CHAPTER TWO

1. Rudine Sims Bishop, "Author Quotes," *Good Reads*, https://www.goodreads.com/author/quotes/170243.Rudine_Sims_Bishop.
2. Harvey Daniels, *Literature Circles: Voice and Choice in Book Clubs and Reading Groups*, 2nd ed. (Portsmouth: Stenhouse, 2002).

CHAPTER THREE

1. Oscar Hammerstein, "Getting to Know You," Sound Track Lyrics, accessed March 6, 2020, http://www.stlyrics.com/lyrics/thekingandi/gettingtoknowyou.htm.
2. Council of Writing Program Administrators, "WPA Outcomes Statement for First-Year Composition (3.0)," https://wpacouncil.org/aws/CWPA/pt/sd/news_article/243055/_PARENT/layout_details/false.
3. Ralph Ellison, "Hidden Name and Complex Fate," in *Shadow and Act* (New York: Random House, Inc, 1964), 148.

4. Sandra Cisneros, "My Name," in *The House on Mango Street* (New York: Vintage, 1991).

5. Richard E. Kim, *Lost Names: Scenes from a Korean Boyhood*, 2nd ed. (Oakland: University of California Press, 2011); Thea Halo, *Not Even My Name* (New York: Picador, 2001); and Jhumpa Lahiri, *The Namesake: A Novel*, reprint ed. (Boston: Mariner Books, 2004).

CHAPTER FOUR

1. Robert Newton Peck, *A Day No Pigs Would Die* (New York: Alfred A. Knopf, 1972), 18–19.

2. California Reading and Literature Project (CRLP) participants, *Literature for All Students: A Sourcebook for Teachers* (Sacramento: California Department of Education, 1985).

3. Margy Burns Knight and Anne Sibley O'Brien, *Talking Walls* (Thomaston, ME: Tilbury House Publishers, 1992).

4. Robert Frost, "Mending Wall," in *North of Boston* (London: David Nutt, 1914).

5. Angela Moore and the NCTE Secondary Section Steering Committee, "The Framing Routine: What Is It and Why Should You Try It with Your Students?," https://ncte.org/blog/2021/05/framing-routine-try-students/.

6. Gary D. Schmidt, *The Wednesday Wars*, reprint ed. (New York: Clarion Books, 2009).

CHAPTER FIVE

1. Elizabeth Borton de Treviño, *I, Juan de Pareja* (New York: Square Fish Books, 2008), 6.

2. Louise Rosenblatt, *The Reader, The Text, and The Poem: The Transactional Theory of the Literary Work*, Paperback ed. (Carbondale: Southern Illinois University Press, 1994).

3. Cris Tovani, *I Read It but Don't Get It: Comprehension Strategies for Adolescent Readers* (Portsmouth, NH: Stenhouse Publishers, 2000).

4. Susan Zimmermann and Chryse Hutchins, *Seven Keys to Comprehension: How to Help Your Kids Read It and Get It*, self-published (Harmony, 2003).

5. Fran Claggett and Joan Brown, *Drawing Your Own Conclusions: Graphic Strategies for Reading, Writing, and Thinking* (Portsmouth, NH: Heinemann, 1992).

6. *Houghton Mifflin College Dictionary* (Boston: Houghton Mifflin, 1986), s.v. "poem."

CHAPTER SIX

1. "Genres of Literature," http://genresofliterature.com/.

2. Sarah Hahn Campbell, "More Than Just Writing: Using Research to Connect Again," *English Journal (NCTE)* 112.3 (January 2023): 71–77.

3. Jim Burke, "Teaching the Academic Essentials," PDF file (n.d.), https://www.lcps.org/cms/lib/VA01000195/Centricity/Domain/17518/BurkeHOutsFullWorkshop.pdf.

4. College and Career Readiness Anchor Standards (CCRA.SL.2) Speaking and Listening, Department of Defense Education Activity (DoDEA), https://www.dodea.edu/collegecareerready/ela-standards.cfm?ID=CCR.ELA-Literacy.CCRA.SL&title=College%20and%20Career%20Readiness%20Anchor%20Standards%20for%20Speaking%20and%20Listening.

5. "Five Key Questions of Media Literacy," *Center for Media Literacy* PDF file (2005), https://www.medialit.org/sites/default/files/14B_CCKQPoster+5essays.pdf.

CHAPTER SEVEN

1. Anna J. Small Roseboro, "Words, Words, Words," *Fine Lines* (Spring 2005): 51.

2. "Poetry Resources," National Council of Teachers of English, https://ncte.org/resources/poetry/.

3. Naoshi Koriyama, "Unfolding Bud," https://genius.com/Naoshi-koriyama-unfolding-bud-annotated.

4. Anna J. Small Roseboro, "Poetry T.I.M.E. Introduction to Poetry Analysis," www.teachingenglishlanguagearts.com.

5. Kimberly Athans, "Poetry is a Vibe! Engaging Students with Poetry," *California English*, 28, no. 3 (February 2023): 14.

6. Emily Dickinson, "I'm Nobody! Who are you?" https://poets.org/poem/im-nobody-who-are-you-260.

7. Teresa Bassett, "Paradise Fiction," in *Freeze Frame Fiction*, https://freezeframefiction.com/paradise-city-by-teresa-bassett/.

8. Mark Twain (Samuel Clemens), *The Adventures of Huckleberry Finn and Related Readings* (Evanston, IL: McDougall Littell, 1997), 121–22.

CHAPTER EIGHT

1. Christine Haas and Linda Flower, "Rhetorical Reading Strategies and the Construction of Meaning," *College Composition and Communication*, 39, no. 2 (1988): 168. http://www.jstor.org/stable/358026.

2. Bryan Stevenson, *Just Mercy: A Story of Justice and Redemption* (London: Oneworld Publications, 2014).

Bibliography

Andrade, Heidi Goodrich. "Teaching with Rubrics: The Good, the Bad, and the Ugly." *College Teaching* 53, no. 1 (Winter 2005): 27–30. http://www.jstor.org/stable/27559213.

Athans, Kimberly. "Poetry Is a Vibe! Engaging Students with Poetry." *California English* 28, no. 3 (February 2023): 14.

Bassett, Teresa. "Paradise Fiction." *Freeze Frame Fiction.* https://freezeframefiction.com/paradise-city-by-teresa-basset/.

Bishop, Rudine Sims. "Author Quotes." *Good Reads.* https://www.goodreads.com/author/quotes/170243.Rudine_Sims_Bishop.

Blair, Walter and John Gerber. *Better Reading Two—Literature.* 3rd ed. Chicago: Scott Foresman, 1959.

Burke, Jim. "Teaching Academic Essentials." https://www.lcps.org/cms/lib/VA01000195/Centricity/Domain/17518/BurkeHOutsFullWorkshop.pdf.

California Reading and Literature Project (CRLP) participants. *Literature for All Students: A Sourcebook for Teachers.* Sacramento: California Department of Education, 1985.

Campbell, Sarah Hahn. "More Than Just Writing: Using Research to Connect Again." *English Journal (NCTE)* 112.3 (January 2023): 71–77.

Center for Media Literacy "Five Key Questions of Media Literacy," *Center for Media Literacy* PDF file. (2005). https://www.medialit.org/sites/default/files/14B_CCKQPoster+5essays.pdf

Cisneros, Sandra. "My Name." In *House on Mango Street.* New York: Vintage, 1991.

Claggett, Fran and Joan Brown. *Drawing Your Own Conclusions: Graphic Strategies for Reading, Writing, and Thinking.* Reprint ed. Portsmouth, NH: Heinemann, 1992.

College and Career Readiness Anchor Standards (CCRA.SL.2) Speaking and Listening. Department of Defense Education Activity (DoDEA). https://www.dodea.edu/collegecareerready/ela-standards.cfm?ID=CCR.ELA-Literacy.CCRA.SL&title=College%20and%20Career%20Readiness%20Anchor%20Standards%20for%20Speaking%20and%20Listening.

Collins, Phil. "Son of Man." Soundtrack Lyrics. https://www.stlyrics.com/lyrics/tarzan/sonofman.htm.

Council of Writing Program Administrators. "WPA Outcomes Statement for First-Year Composition (3.0)." https://wpacouncil.org/aws/CWPA/pt/sd/news_article/243055 /_PARENT/layout_details/false.

Curtis, Christopher Paul. *The Watsons Go to Birmingham—1963.* New York: Yearling, 1997.

Daniels, Harvey. *Literature Circles: Voice and Choice in Book Clubs and Reading Groups.* 2nd ed. Portsmouth, NH: Stenhouse, 2002.

de Treviño, Elizabeth Borton. *I, Juan de Pareja.* New York: Square Fish Books, 2008.

Dickinson, Emily. "I'm Nobody! Who are you?" https://poets.org/poem/im-nobody -who-are-you-260.

Ellison, Ralph. "Hidden Name and Complex Fate." In *Shadow and Act.* New York: Random House, Inc., 1964.

Frost, Robert. "Mending Wall." In *North of Boston.* London: David Nutt, 1914. Available at gutenberg.org.

Gardner, Howard. *Frames of Mind: The Theory of Multiple Intelligences.* 3rd ed. New York: Basic Books, 2011.

"Genres of Literature." http://genresofliterature.com/.

Haas, Christine and Linda Flower. "Rhetorical Reading Strategies and the Construction of Meaning." *College Composition and Communication* 39, no. 2 (1988): 168. http: //www.jstor.org/stable/358026.

Halo, Thea. *Not Even My Name: A True Story.* New York: Picador, 2001.

Hammerstein, Oscar. "Getting to Know You." Soundtrack Lyrics. Accessed 6 March 2020. http://www.stlyrics.com/lyrics/thekingandi/gettingtoknowyou.htm.

Kim, Richard E. *Lost Names: Scenes from a Korean Boyhood.* 2nd ed. Oakland, CA: University of California Press, 2011.

Knight, Margy Burns and Anne Sibley O'Brien. *Talking Walls.* Thomaston, ME: Tilbury House Publishers, 1992.

Lahiri, Jumpha. *The Namesake: A Novel.* Reprint ed. Boston: Mariner Books, 2004.

Mintz, Steven. "How to Improve College Teaching in 2023." *Higher Ed Gamma* (blog). Inside Higher Ed. 9 January 2023. https://www.insidehighered.com/blogs/ higher-ed-gamma/how-improve-college-teaching-2023.

Moore, Angela and the NCTE Secondary Section Steering Committee. "The Framing Routine: What Is It and Why Should You Try It with Your Students?" https://ncte .org/blog/2021/05/framing-routine-try-students/.

Morrison, Toni. *The Bluest Eye.* Vintage International ed. New York: Knopf Doubleday, 2007.

National Council of Teachers of English. "Poetry Resources." https://ncte.org/ resources/poetry/.

Peck, Robert Newton. *A Day No Pigs Would Die.* New York: Alfred A. Knopf, 1972.

Roseboro, Anna J. Small. "Words, Words, Words." *Fine Lines* (Spring 2005): 51.

Rosenblatt, Louise. *The Reader, The Text, and The Poem: The Transactional Theory of the Literary Work.* Paperback ed. Carbondale: Southern Illinois University Press, 1994.

Sands, Gayle. "Word Play for August." https://www.ethicalela.com/wordplay-for -august/.

Schmidt, Gary D. *The Wednesday Wars*. Reprint ed. New York: Clarion Books, 2009.

Stevenson, Bryan. *Just Mercy: A Story of Justice and Redemption*. London: Oneworld Publications, 2014.

Tovani, Cris. *I Read It, but I Don't Get It: Comprehension Strategies for Adolescent Readers*. Portsmouth, NH: Stenhouse Publishers, 2000.

Twain, Mark (Samuel Clemens). *The Adventures of Huckleberry Finn and Related Readings*, 121–22. Evanston, IL: McDougall Littell, 1997.

White, Edward M. "My Five-Paragraph-Theme Theme." https://ubcompositionsummer2013.files.wordpress.com/2013/05/white-my-five-paragraph-theme-theme.pdf.

Woodson, Jaqueline. *Brown Girl Dreaming*. Illustrated ed. New York: Nancy Paulsen Books, 2016.

Zimmerman, Susan and Chryse Hutchins. *Seven Keys to Comprehension: How to Help Your Kids Read It and Get It*. Self-published. Harmony, 2003.

About the Authors
and Contributors

Anna J. Small Roseboro, a wife, mother, and National Board-Certified Teacher has over four decades of experience teaching in public, parochial, and private schools and colleges, mentoring early career educators, and facilitating leadership institutes. She has taught students in five different states across the country, served as director of summer school programs, coached an award-winning competitive speech team, and chaired her English department. Anna represented Rotary International in a group-study exchange with educators in East Africa.

She has authored books in multiple genres: fiction, poetry, and textbooks for teachers. She has tutored adult English-language learners with the Literacy Center of Michigan. The California Association of Teachers of English (2009) and the National Council of Teachers of English (2016) each awarded her their Distinguished Service Award. In 2021, the Michigan Council of Teachers of English awarded her their Teacher of Excellence Award. Anna now serves as director emeritus of the Early Career Educators of Color Leadership Award Program and as a mentor with the National Board for Professional Teaching Standards.

Dr. Susan Steffel, professor emeritus of English at Central Michigan University (CMU), taught both undergraduate and graduate courses in English education and young adult literature. Steffel has served as president of the Michigan Council of Teachers of English, editor of the *Language Arts Journal of Michigan*, and president of the Michigan Conference on English Education. She has written numerous books, chapters, and articles, serves as a reviewer for state and national professional journals, is a frequent conference presenter, and continues to work with classroom teachers providing professional development. Susan is a founding codirector of the Chippewa River Writing Project at CMU. Her commitment to helping others is demonstrated through her many professional responsibilities, including her work as a mentor for English educators at both the state and national levels and as an English language-arts consultant. Most recently, she collaborated as a cofounder of the MCTE Stephens-Brown-Steffel (SBS) Award Recognizing Outstanding Literature for Young Adults with a Michigan connection.

Some of her professional awards and honors include twice receiving the CMU College of Humanities and Social and Behavioral Science Excellence in Teaching Award and the Michigan Council of Teachers of English Charles Carpenter Fries Award and being named a CMU Faculty Center for Innovative Teaching Fellow and the Michigan Distinguished Professor of the Year by the President's Council of State Universities of Michigan. In addition, she twice received the CMU Excellence in Teaching Award.

WE, ANNA AND SUSAN, THANK
OUR CONTRIBUTORS

Kimberly Athans, professor of education, School of Education, Point Loma Nazarene University, Point Loma, California

Stefani Boutelier, associate professor of education, Aquinas College, Grand Rapids, Michigan

Earl H. Brooks, assistant professor of English, University of Maryland, Baltimore County, Maryland

Jim Burke, English teacher, mentor, and author, Burlingame, California

Sarah Hahn Campbell, English teacher, South High School, Denver, Colorado

José Luis Cano Jr., doctoral candidate, department of English, Texas Christian University, Dallas-Fort Worth, Texas

Shanika P. Carter, adjunct professor, department of English, Grand Valley State University, Allendale, Michigan

DuValle Daniel, English professor, Shoreline Community College, Shoreline, Washington

Esther Gabay, English professor, Community College, New York, New York

Mara Lee Grayson, assistant professor of English, California State University, Dominguez Hills, California

Cheryl Hogue Smith, professor of English, Kingsborough Community College, CUNY, Brooklyn, New York

Jessica Hudson, visiting professor, Principia College, Elsah, Illinois

Nancy G. (Perkins) Kohl, veteran educator, adjunct faculty, University of Massachusetts, Lowell, Massachusetts

Kia Jane Richmond, professor, English education program director, Northern Michigan University, Marquette, Michigan

Rosalyn Roz Roseboro, adjunct professor, writing department, Grand Valley State University, Allendale, Michigan

Gayle Sands, professional development school liaison, McDaniel College, Westminster, Maryland

Alison (Fastov) Taylor, veteran English educator, mentor, former teacher at Georgetown Day School, Washington, DC

Anna White, Library Scholars Program faculty mentor, Grand Valley State University, Allendale, Michigan

See contributor photos on the next two pages.

Kimberly Athans
Pt. Loma Nazarene U
Point Loma, CA

Stefani Boutelier
Aquinas College
Grand Rapids, MI

Earl Brooks
University of Maryland
Baltimore, MD

Jim Burke
College of San Matea
Burlingame, CA

Sarah Hahn Campbell
South High School
Denver, CO

Jose Luis Cano
Texas Christian College
Fort Worth, TX

Shanika Carter
Grand Valley State U
Allendale, MI

DuValle Daniel
Shoreline CC
Shoreline, WA

Esther Gabay
Community College
New York, NY

Mara Lee Grayson
Cal State University
Dominguez Hills CA

Cheryl Hogue Smith
Kingsborough CC
Brooklyn, NY

Jessica Hudson
Principia College
Elsah, IL

Nancy (Perkins) Kohl
Univ. of Massachusetts
Lowell, MA

Kia Richmond
Northern Michigan U
Marquette, MI

Rosalyn (Roz) Roseboro
Grand Valley State. U
Allendale, MI

Gayle J. Sands
McDaniel College
Westminster, MA

Alison (Fastov) Taylor
Georgetown Day Sch
Washington, DC

Anna White
Grand Valley St. U
Allendale, MI

Printed in Great Britain
by Amazon

56829790R00106